FLYING HIGH

Helen MacKay and her husband fly from Nova Scotia to the land of their forebears. The first stop is London, where the Tower, Buckingham Palace, and the Cockney lingo prove rather overpowering. Then on to Scotland — 'from Loch to Loch and Ben to Ben' — but underneath the breezy style and humour lies an awareness of the magic of these isles, and as she so truly writes: 'After Scotland anything was bound to be an anti-climax'.

FLYING HIGH

HELEN F. MACKAY

Illustrated
by
REDMOND CURTIS

ARTHUR H. STOCKWELL LTD.
Elms Court Ilfracombe
Devon

First published in Great Britain, 1971

SBN 7223 0231 - 2
PRINTED IN GREAT BRITAIN BY
ARTHUR H. STOCKWELL LTD.
Elms Court - Ilfracombe
Devon

ILLUSTRATIONS

"As in the wanderings of Ulysses, I had seen many unusual things, *mirabile dictu*, including monsters of the deep, enchanted castles, snakes that did not exist, a fabulous smoo, and reeling rivers."

This book is dedicated to my daughter, Maura, who encouraged me by laughing at my attempts at humour and thus was indirectly responsible for its infliction on the public.

CHAPTER I

The Captain's voice came over the loudspeaker: "We are now cruising at an altitude of 32,500 feet; the temperature outside is 60 degrees below zero." We were flying high; some of the passengers, indeed, were quite high, due to the cumulative effects of a get-acquainted party at the Nova Scotian Hotel prior to our take-off, followed by a succession of cocktails, champagne, liqueurs and what-have-you ever since the bar on the plane opened. As these drinks were free most people seemed to feel that they had a moral obligation to imbibe as many as possible as quickly as possible.

This was our first trip across the Atlantic for my husband and myself. He had been recently retired and we were both now entering what you might call our 'golden years'. I am not quite sure what that means but it is a euphonious phrase very much in vogue of late and I suspect it means 'slightly doddering'.

For weeks I had planned carefully as to what to take in the way of clothes. On the advice of friends who had been to Europe and were consequently in the know, I packed wispy nylon undies and drip-dry shirts and blouses. On the advice of other friends, equally knowing, I stowed woollen snuggies, my husband's long underwear and innumerable heavy sweaters, for they assured me that we would freeze, "simply freeze, with no central heating, you know".

I managed to contain all this diversified apparel in two very bulging flight bags, which presumably were now accompanying us to London. One thing I abhor is to be burdened with a lot of impedimenta while travelling so I had simply my handbag with me to look after.

After we were air-borne for a short time, my husband attempted to adjust his chair to a more comfortable angle but found that it did not respond to any amount of button pushing; it insisted on remaining upright, in fact it seemed inclined almost at a forward angle. He mentioned this to the stewardess as she came by and she tried to adjust it but without success, whereupon she promised to send someone who would look after it.

As time went by and the 'someone' never materialized, we waylaid, at intervals, any of the plane personnel who happened to pass by and each, in turn, assured us that it would be attended to immediately. In spite of all these assurances, however, my husband remained folded up like an accordian throughout the night and breathing down the neck of the lady in front of him.

As she reclined at ease in her seat she was blissfully unaware that her chances of receiving an unsolicited Scotch and soda, applied externally to her person, were definitely more than minimal.

My husband is a patient man, the type who puts up with things rather than make a fuss, but even he had the urge to kill when, towards morning when breakfast was being served, the stewardess said brightly to him: "Wouldn't you care to put your seat back and relax?"

Undoubtedly some sort of record for bridging the Atlantic was established that night and my husband is entitled to due recognition as I am convinced that he is the first to make a jack-knife crossing.

But in any position, whether comfortable or not, sleep was impossible. In addition to the usual noise of the jet, as the night advanced there was a rising *crescendo* of voices as is customary in all well-oiled cocktail parties.

The lady sitting next to me had a stertorian voice at normal range but when she upped it a few decibels in an effort to be heard, the effect would have been ear-shattering on the average individual. But I endured it with comparative equanimity. After all I had spent my youth in a rugged coastal village where my ears had become conditioned by the sudden blasts of a nearby fog-horn. I was thankful now for my virtually shatter-proof ear drums. In spite of all that, we did our best to carry on polite conversation – she bellowing at me and I, in turn, screaming at her.

All this time we had been flying miles up over a vast 'meringue pie', but suddenly the topping seemed to thin out a bit and we could obtain glimpses of yellows, pale greens and pastel pinks which, after closer scrutiny, proved to be England.

Throughout the night we seemed to have been just chugging along, barely moving so it seemed, but now, at last, we really felt that we were jet flying. As the countryside sped away underneath us, I was sure that we were going to end somewhere in the North Sea. But the pilot, stout fellow that he was, apparently had very fixed ideas of his own and, without even a detour to Cuba, went unerringly to his established destination and, in a matter of minutes, deposited his craft and contents thereof joltlessly on the tarmac.

When we emerged from our safe cocoon we were on our own in London Airport. As crowds were dashing in all directions, we revved up our personal motors and sprinted along, not knowing exactly where we were headed. I may explain that the word 'sprinted' as far as I am concerned means that I achieved a brisk waddle.

First we had to present our passports so, going along with the time-worn adage of safety in numbers, we joined a long queue of people who seemed to know what they were doing. After about twenty minutes of slow progress towards the wicket, the uneasy thought presented itself to my sluggish brain that we were in the wrong line-up.

I carefully reread the various headings in evidence: Domestic, Foreign, United Kingdom, Republic of Eire, Commonwealth of Australia, U.S. Citizens, and others which I have forgotten. Now the task of sorting oneself out under one or other of these classifications is not easy, especially after a sleepless night. I was not naïve enough to expect that there would be a special wicket headed 'Cape Bretoners' (although that would be only their rightful due) or even 'Nova Scotians', but you would think they would have heard of Canadians, especially after *EXPO* and all that.

While I was mentally debating whether we should move over to the American queue as, after all, we were Americans in the larger meaning of the term, an official yanked us out of line and thrust us at the end of another column where we started the forward process all over again. We were now in the 'Foreign' line-up, but by this time I did not much care how they chose to classify us; they could have put us under 'Aborigines' and I would not have disputed them.

Eventually we confronted the inspector and duly presented our passports. My husband got through without incident, but when the inspector scrutinized my passport photo, a perceptible shudder ran through his frame. I could truly understand his reaction as I found myself experiencing much the same whenever I had occasion to produce my passport and my gaze would inadvertently encounter the unreasonable facsimile affixed thereon.

We now had to locate our luggage and get through Customs. An endless conveyor belt brings up the various pieces of luggage and they travel around on a revolving platform from which they are snatched by their owners. After anxiously watching about 3,000 heterogeneous pieces make their appearance, circling slowly in front of us like fashion models on a ramp, I was ready to give up all hope of ever being reunited with my own lowly luggage, when behold, the last piece was mine, and riding along very companionably with it was my husband's flight bag.

There are times such as this when you simply have to carry your own luggage so my husband made a dive for the two pieces. Although one of them alone would have been a good weight for any man to carry, he, with indisputable masculine logic, maintained that it was just as easy to carry the two, the idea being that the weight on one side would nullify the weight on the other.

The customs official presented no problem. Nevertheless, he left me with the uneasy sensation that I had slipped up on a matter of protocol. He asked: "Are you bringing over any gifts?" When I replied in the negative, he looked so disapproving that I realized I was expected to bring gifts to somebody. When I tried to explain that I knew nobody in England, he dismissed me politely but firmly. Perhaps, on my first visit to England, I was expected to bring some little gift to the Queen, maybe something typical of our Province, say, a salt cod or a blueberry pie. However, it was much too late to do anything about it then so we proceeded to locate a taxi.

This entailed standing in a queue again for another longish interval before we finally acquired one. When the driver turned to me and said "Where to, luv?" I realized that at last we were in London.

CHAPTER II

The Atlantic Crossing had taken five hours, but from the time we landed at London Airport until we reached our hotel almost three hours had elapsed. At this stage we were in no mood for anything but a little rest and sleep. After registering we looked around for a porter but there was none in evidence so my husband and I along with another couple who were travelling with us decided not to wait but took our bags and baggage to the elevator.

When I proceeded to step to the rear of the lift as I generally do, I found myself banging painfully into a wall and I realized that the lift was approximately 18 inches in depth, although a mirror on the rear wall helped to foster the delusion of size. Now when you attempt to compress four people plus four flight bags along with various other items into a space adequate for two, you find yourself bucking the old law of Physics about matter occupying space.

The thought occurred to me at the time that the phenomenon known as 'Twiggy' was perhaps a subconscious effort on the part of the British to fit the people to the lifts rather than *vice versa.*

I noticed that English lifts, besides being diminutive

possess very little patience. You step lively getting in or out or else! He who hesitates is lost or at least decapitated. Of course you could keep your finger on the 'Hold' button to delay the closing of the door, but again this involves a certain amount of gymnastics. You have your arm inside with your finger on the button, while the rest of you is out and around the corner and half-way down the corridor.

Later on, during my stay at this particular hotel, I actually did encounter the porter, thus verifying the fact that there was such a thing. When I got in the lift he was there obviously taking some luggage somewhere. When he stopped at his floor he asked if I would mind holding the lift as he would be right back. This I was glad to do because, after all, we must present a good Canadian image while abroad, so I dutifully kept my thumb on the button and waited . . . and waited . . . and waited. As my digit gradually lost all sensation I felt like you-know-who at the dyke. I decided finally that it was plumb dumb to get a numb thumb just to foster international goodwill: "To heck with it" said I to myself in Gaelic and I went my separate way. I never did see him again.

Our room at the hotel was more than adequate. It had apparently been recently done over in the modern manner with beautiful drapes and carpeting. The adjoining bathroom was quite large with french windows opening on a stone parapet, where countless pigeons disported themselves with much billing and cooing as such birds are wont to do. As there were no screens on the windows the prospect of having several of these pigeons join me in my bath seemed more than a remote possibility. However, as time went on, I realized that they had been well trained in proper bird decorum and never ventured beyond their prescribed limits.

In the evening of our first day in London (sounds like the Book of Genesis) we roused from our slumbers and set out to conquer the City. The first thing to be done in any strange place is to find out where you are before you try to get where you're not. Accordingly we acquired a map of London and pin-pointed ourselves on it. When we discovered that we were just a block or two away from Piccadilly Circus, we made that our first objective.

It all seemed very simple. All we had to do was walk around a block and then turn left – or so we thought. In the first place in London you do not walk around a block and get back to where you started. There are no such things as right angles. Even Euclid would be at a loss to find one. There are all sorts of acute angles and hundreds of obtuse ones but no right angles. Nothing is more confusing than to follow an obtusing angle; you end up miles away from where you expected to be.

Moreover, to add to the general befuddlement of tourists, streets are constantly changing their names; they are temperamental and undependable; they change their names every few blocks, or so it seems; they criss-cross, back-track, turn at unbelievable angles or stop abruptly never to be heard of again.

And so it was that on our first evening in London we walked for miles in every conceivable direction in an effort to reach Piccadilly Circus. Finally I could take it no longer; I was all in, I was exhausted, I was completely and utterly spent and what's more I was slightly fatigued so I sat myself down on a nearby curb and rested.

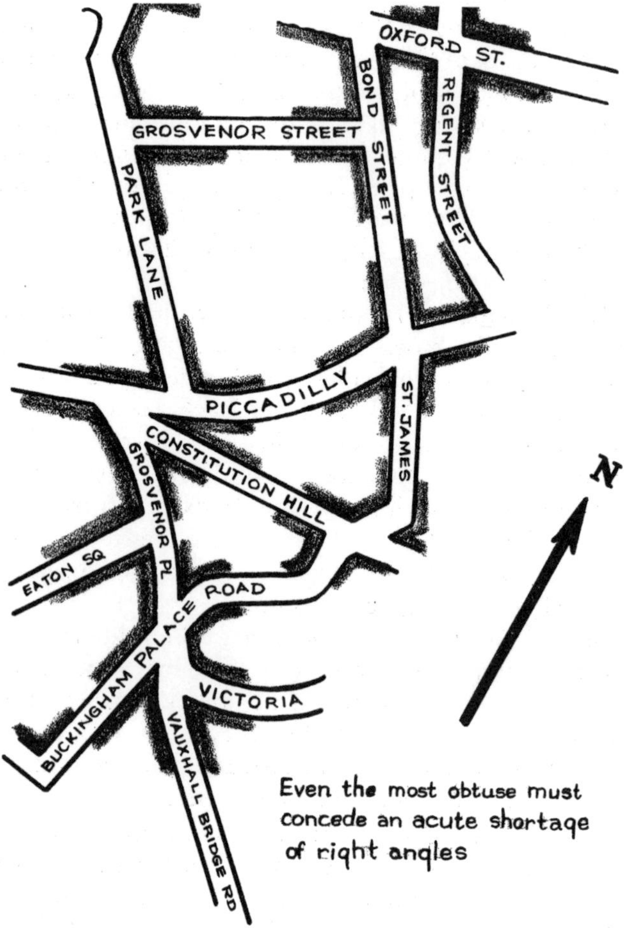

Even the most obtuse must concede an acute shortage of right angles

When I had recovered myself sufficiently to be aware of my environment, I heard strains of music and the splashing of water from a fountain. Above the fountain rose the statue of Eros and here I was in Piccadilly Circus.

The odd looking specimens I saw grouped around the fountain were not gargoyles but hippies, as I found out later that this was their favourite rendezvous. Several of the less comatose ones were playing guitars but the remainder were simply resting having presumably attained Nirvana. I was inclined to envy them; while the traffic roared by they were in a little peaceful oasis of their own. I wondered whether they would welcome a tottering old lady to their ranks.

I caught a glimpse of my husband and tried to attract his attention but he strode doggedly by. In a few minutes, however, he apparently sensed that he was missing something, namely me, for he retraced his steps and located me in the hippy domain. He seemed to be a bit irate. Whether that was due to the fact that he had been unable to find me for a while or, as is more probable, to the fact that he did locate me, I shall never be quite certain.

The pace for the next few days varied from the frenzied to the frenetic. We had three days to 'sight-see' London so we hurriedly drew up a list of things that our friends back home would expect us to see, namely the Tower of London, Madame Tussaud's Wax Works, Buckingham Palace, Windsor Castle, Hampton Court, and others.

Our next problem was to get to these places. Being imbued with the spirit of adventure we decided to try the subway. We were told that the nearest entrance to the underground was just around the corner, so we walked half a mile or so before we finally found it. After that the rest was easy. We had merely to go down a flight of stairs, turn right, go down an escalator, turn left, walk a hundred feet or so, turn right again and get on the train which was just pulling in. Sorry – wrong train! But we were already on it and it was speeding on its way – which was not our way.

We got off at the next stop, walked a hundred feet or so, went up a flight of stairs, turned left, then right, then straight ahead until we came to an elevator, got on the elevator and it took us to the surface where we were ejected into the street.

Whereupon, we had to walk around the block a few times until we found the entrance back into the subway. Then we paid a second admission fee, walked a quarter of a mile down a corridor, went down a flight of stairs, turned right, walked around in a circle for a while just to get our bearings, went down another escalator (the longest and steepest in the world, I heard later and I believe it), turned a few more corners and there we were, staggering on our train with no trouble at all. I had just time to draw a deep breath when we were all out again. There is no doubt that the London Tube is fast – it is the getting in and out that takes the time.

After that experience, when we discovered we were headed in the wrong direction, we found that it was better not to back-track but to emerge at whatever station sounded interesting. In this way we 'sight-saw' many places not on our list but we also saved a lot of valuable time.

In spite of my determination to carry only a hand-bag, I found myself encumbered with a camera, a raincoat, a tote bag and finally an umbrella. This last I purchased in London after I noticed that practically everyone in the City carried one. Now, where I come from, the umbrella, although not really extinct, has had its numbers seriously depleted of late years. Most men would scorn the idea of taking an umbrella in case of rain, as they fancy themselves as rugged he-men impervious to all vicissitudes of weather. As for the teenager the idea would be completely ridiculous.

I was amused, therefore, at the sight of a hippie, with his long, unkempt, unwashed hair, and clothed in a miscellaneous collection of discards, bravely holding up an umbrella to ward off a few scattered drops of rain. The incident inspired me to indite the following hydrophobic effusion:

I do not blame a fella
For toting an umbrella
When it's drippy,

but

A little bit of water
Is something that had oughter
Help a hippie.

CHAPTER III

After one of our haphazard sorties from the Underground, we found ourselves in front of the Tower of London, so we decided that it was as good a time as any to absorb a little bit of history. To my surprise I found that the Tower is not just one tower but consists of a number of towers. This is probably a typical example of the British propensity to understatement. There are the Bell Tower, the White Tower, the Wakefield Tower, the 'Sanguineous' Tower and others that I cannot recall at the moment. In case you have never heard of the last mentioned tower, I must explain that the name by which it is commonly known was considered indelicate in my day so I am taking the liberty of renaming it by applying a more refined synonym. I am determined not to lower my standards at this late date.

By some happy circumstance the Tower has obligingly situated itself on the banks of the Thames, thus facilitating the heave-hoing of dead bodies, and some not so dead, from the turrets into the river. That was, of course, in days of yore. Today the procedure is much more subtle – they merely walk you to death. You ambulate, you peregrinate and you pursue a peripatetic course up endless flights of stairs and presumably down an equal number, through vast corridors and chambers filled with all sorts of interesting artifacts.

There are swords, rapiers, pistols, lances, maces, spears, javelins, cross-bows, slings and arrows of outrageous fortune and many other instruments of vivisection, as practised in the good old days when Knighthood was in flower.

In the Armoury room the Knights were posing like manikins while they displayed the latest thing in male attire in vogue in their particular era. One very chic number which caught my eye was designated as 'skirted armour'. It consisted of a riveted metallic plate mini-skirt in the A line worn over leggings with bulbous knees. The bodice was of simple design showing a shawl effect collar. With this costume matching helmet and gauntlets were worn.

Another little model which appealed to me was the 'Pikeman'. This was apparently for casual wear rather than formal. Again the metallic mini-skirt was featured, but this time it was fashioned in the bouffant style and was worn over a pair of plus-fours. On the head was worn a dashing metal hat somewhat resembling a fisherman's sou'wester. To complete the ensemble the model bore in his hand a pike. A pike in this instance is not a fish but is a long pointed rod which was probably used for spearing eels.

It is hard to imagine a knight, encased in one of these suits of armour, calling on his lady love. But obviously it was not designed for pitching woo or smooching or whatever the current term is. The knights, from what I can learn, did not engage in such amorous pursuits but spent all their time jousting and tilting and these activities, whatever they were, apparently demanded formal dress. A coat of mail was definitely *de rigeur.*

As I looked around at all the armour on display, I could not help but wonder whether any of these suits were occupied. In other words, was there a knight in shining armour? Perhaps the odd one had been inadvertently overlooked over the centuries and was rattling around inside in a dessicated sort of way. Such things can happen. I was tempted to raise a visor here and there and peer in. But then, what if I should see something peering out at me? This contingency, even though remote, proved so unnerving that I hastily withdrew from the Tower and betook myself to a nearby tea-room.

I have always found that in times of great mental stress there is nothing so soothing as a cup of tea; and in the British Isles they serve you tea that is tea. They invariably put in front of you a large teapot holding at least three cups, and another pot containing hot water along with a generous pitcher of milk.

In this instance, however, I was disappointed to find that the tea was not hot. When I brought this to the attention of the waitress – a genial soul with a Cockney accent – she promptly inserted her finger in the cup of tea and after giving it a stir or two remarked: "Lord, luv, it is cold; that's what comes of having a man make it." She promptly whisked off the offending teapot and soon returned with one that really was piping hot.

When I had sufficiently recovered from my nervous strain and my hands had stopped shaking, I returned to the Tower in order to see the Crown Jewels. I joined the lengthy queue and slowly snaked and slithered forward until finally I was able to view briefly (because we had to keep moving) the various crowns, orbs, ampullas, swords and salts all adorned with fabulous jewels. The salts interested me. After an involved process of deductive reasoning, I concluded that these were containers for holding salt. I tried to visualize myself shaking a little salt on my morning egg from a container two feet high, made of solid gold and built in the form of a castle.

The picture seemed somehow unrealistic so I moved along until in scintillating brilliancy in front of me was the biggest cut diamond in the world. 'The Star of Africa', set in the Royal Sceptre. It was so large it was unbelievable. I found myself looking for comparison at the pin-point diamond on my left hand. And as I looked I felt a vast surge of anger rising within me – to think that this apology for a diamond was the best my husband could do for me – the piker. I resolved that I would not speak to him for a week, but not that week. I would wait until I returned home, when I would have more time for not speaking and could give the matter my full and undivided attention.

That afternoon we betook ourselves to Madame Tussaud's Wax Works, then to the Planetarium, which was next door and finally to Regents Park, just a short distance away.

At the entrance to the wax works we made an error common to many people of thinking that the guard standing there was real. It was an embarrassing mistake but it was not nearly as unsettling as what occurred later on in the Chamber of Horrors. As it happened I was standing quite still, apparently in a state of suspended animation, when some tourist, mistaking me for a 'horror', poked me with an inquisitive finger in an effort to verify whether I was human or not. After that gruesome experience it was a relief to be wafted around in cosmic space at the Planetarium and above all, to be able to sit down for a while.

It is impossible to go very far in London without running headlong into a park and that is what happened to us after our trip through outer space. It was an unplanned but extremely pleasant interlude as we roamed through the beautifully land-scaped grounds of Regents Park. We were impressed with the profusion of flowers and the waterways with their swans, ducks and other birds, and people in punts.

Our Canadian parks are generally equipped with sedate, dignified and mostly uncomfortable benches set at discreet intervals along a walk and there are always numerous signs warning the public to *arcite gramen.* (I am just showing off my high school Latin). But there were no such signs in Regents Park that I could see. I am quite sure that if you inadvertently stumbled and fell anywhere in the park, you would automatically find yourself reclining at ease in a lawn chair – and what a delightful place to snooze away a drowsy afternoon.

But such soporific inducements were not for us. There were snaps to be taken before sunset and tea to be quaffed (or is it ale that is quaffed?) in the Red Rose Tea Garden that we had spotted near the entrance. As usual the tea was excellent. We sat in the open at a little table in a bower of roses whose scent filled the air. The sun went down in the western sky as it is wont to do and the big city seemed very, very remote.

Whether it was due to the stimulation of the tea or to incipient second childhood or just to sore feet, I removed my shoes and went cavorting barefoot on the greensward. You might think that such a spectacle would attract attention as being rather incongrous. But nothing attracts attention in London; the unusual is normal. Anyway the barefoot business was most refreshing to the pedal extremities and we wandered, it seemed, for miles over velvet lawns and along flower bordered walks.

It was then approaching dusk and the park was almost deserted as far as we could see. The terrain was becoming more rugged for on our right was a section of woodland in its natural state. In the deepening gloom a movement in the underbrush caught my eye and I was horrified to note the sinister form of a wolf approaching me with slavering jaws intent on a kill. There were others in the pack too, timber wolves, they were everywhere. Coming from Canada I naturally knew all about these dread animals. With great presence of mind I quietly stepped back a foot or two from the heavy wire fence that enclosed them and peered at the overhead sign that read 'London Zoo'.

I love zoos but this one was mostly closed up and put away for the night so we decided to return another day. We started back to our original entrance in our usual circumambient fashion, losing and finding ourselves a dozen times before we made it. It takes practice to be so stupid.

CHAPTER IV

The following morning, despite creaking bones and protesting muscles, we set out on a tour, a sort of amphibian tour, first by land and then by water. From the comfortable seats of a sight-seeing coach we viewed the suburbs of London and then the pleasant country landscape. What impressed me greatly were the gardens; flowers were planted in every available space and apparently not a weed dared to grow there. I pictured ruefully our own scraggy garden and shaggy lawn back home and the comparison was depressing. I consoled myself, however, with the thought that these English were puttering around their flower plots and gardens a century ago, at which time we Canadians were busily engaged in trying to avoid being scalped by the Indians.

The first stop on our tour was made at Stoke Poges, where we visited St. Giles church in the country churchyard made famous by Gray's Elegy. Although the day was bright and sunny, nevertheless there seemed to be an indescribable atmosphere of melancholy gloom pervading the place. As I stood in the yew tree's shade, the same tree mentioned by the poet and which is now nearly 1,000 years old, I, too, felt impelled to elegize thus:

The curfew tolls the knell of parting day,
The tourists come to see what they can see;
In hushed and solemn tones I hear them pray,
"O Lord, my feet are nearly killing me".

The second portion of the tour was by ferry down the Thames. It was a lovely, lazy, lethargic day and we journeyed along in slow motion, passing now and then through a lock of which there seemed to be quite a number along the course of the river. That appears to be an idiosyncracy of locks, they are almost invariably found along rivers or waterways and are seldom, if ever, seen on dry land. Many beautiful estates came into view, also boat club houses with small craft at anchor on the river.

When our guide informed us that it was pleasure boats such as these that took part in the evacuation at Dunkirk, his simple statement thrilled me more than all the stories of blood and thunder that I had been subjected to at the Tower of London. It is a saga that will never be forgotten. I was so overcome at the time by patriotic fervour that, in spite of my Scottish ancestry, I stood up and started to sing "There'll always be an England". The results were not quite what I had expected. My voice, I will admit, was a wee bit rasping but that was no reason why the pilot should suddenly dock the ferry and put us all ashore.

By some strange coincidence our coach was waiting for us so we en-coached and, merry wives that we were (plus husbands), off we went to Windsor.

After an excellent lunch at the Castle Hotel we

felt strengthened sufficiently to attack Windsor Castle, which stood conveniently nearby. The Castle is situated on quite an eminence overlooking a beautiful stretch of country. Old William the Conqueror was a great picker-outer of sites for castles. It was he who built the Round Tower. At least the lower half of the present structure dates from 1170 A.D. The upper half was just an afterthought, quite a while after in fact, about 1830. As you may have guessed by this time, the Round Tower is, of course, not round. That is just another example of the peculiarities of British nomenclature.

I had expected to see a moat around the Tower, that is a moat with water in it but evidently the aquatic moat is *passé*. That saddened me a little – just another illusion shattered.

Might not a moat be mighty miffed
at finding that his fill
Of water had been cut off 'cause
he hadn't paid his bill?

We were given a little over an hour in which to view the State apartments, including the Queen's Audience Chamber, the Grand Reception Room, the Grand Vestibule, the Waterloo Chamber and many others. My mind, being of limited capacity is simply not geared for absorbing in one hour what required centuries to produce so I can tell you nothing that would be at all enlightening or instructive.

The overall impression I was left with was one of cold magnificence. It is hard to imagine the rooms warming up and getting that lived-in look. I wondered just how they were heated as there seemed to be no evidence of central heating – just elaborate fireplaces.

Frankly, I strongly suspect that the normal temperature of any Englishman is considerably below that of any other so-called warm blooded animals, probably around 92 or 93 degrees. This would enable him to be quite comfortable under near frigid conditions.

There is something to be said in favour of their ancient and endearing custom of pouring boiling tar from the battlements upon their enemies. At least this ensured that some of the people were warm some of the time.

However these are mundane matters and, no doubt, the powers that be in England have everything well in hand so there is no need for me to concern myself about them.

Then on to Hampton Court, a 'super-dooper' palace, the brain child of Cardinal Woolsey, who later was persuaded to pass it over to Henry VIII.

In the Clock Tower a feature of interest was the astronomical clock, which, as I recall, can tell you practically anything you want to know – the forerunner of the computer. It shows the signs of the Zodiac; tells the days of the week, in case you have forgotten them; the phases of the moon; the height of the tidal bore of the Peticodiac, also your age and marital status at the time of the last solar eclipse. Incidentally, it also tells the time.

The State rooms of the Palace were divided into 'His' and 'Hers' by William and Mary, who were dual monarchs way back when. The King's rooms faced south and the Queen's rooms faced east, thus ensuring that they would seldom have to face one another.

The King had his own stairs complete with a magnificent wrought iron balustrade. The walls and ceilings were adorned with an assortment of gods and their female counterparts in various stages of dishabille. All in all it was a very handsome staircase. Presumably the Queen remained upstairs as, short of sliding down the bannister, there seemed to be no provision made for her descent.

Then followed a succession of rooms, each one seemingly more ornate than the last: the King's Drawing Room, the Queen's Gallery, the First Presence Chamber, the Second Presence Chamber, the Audience Chamber and the Royal Chamber Pot. This last was circular in shape with a motif of English roses on the sides and top.

The Haunted Gallery was particularly interesting as it is the abode of the ghost of Catherine Howard, Henry VIII's fifth wife. She is the one who, according to the song, "walks the gloomy corridors at night with her 'ead tucked underneath her arm". Now that story, I, being a sensible person, do not credit for one moment. After all, why should she carry her head under her arm when it would be much more convenient to carry it in a shopping bag?

Our guide for this tour was a very knowledgeable chap who seemed to know everything about everything. Part of his lore I am convinced he attained by divine inspiration. At regular intervals he stood quite immobile, pointed his closed umbrella skyward as though invoking supernatural aid and remained in a trance-like attitude for a minute or so. This was our signal to gather around him and listen to the words of wisdom which fell from his lips.

But somehow or other we became detached from

our prophet and his followers and found ourselves wandering alone in the wilderness. From being bedazzled we became befuddled and roamed about in a futile search for our lost brethren. Eventually we found ourselves at the entrance to a Maze. This is a diabolical device guaranteed to get anyone who enters completely addled, if he has not already reached that state. For us it was a knock-out blow. We would have wandered, without doubt, for days in a daze in the maze, were it not for the fact that some kind guard came to our rescue and delivered us safely to our coach, which was just starting to pull out for London.

The following morning we joined some hundreds of other gawking tourists lined up in front of Buckingham Palace, awaiting the changing of the guard. The guard, presumably, had not proven satisfactory and were to be replaced by others. To my way of thinking this seemed like a rather public way of firing them from their jobs, but that must be the British way of doing things.

There was much fanfare, marching, bands playing, fife and drum, as the guards in scarlet uniform with bearskins on their heads marched to and fro. Apropos of the headgear I have this to say:

The fellow who designed this topper
Was more than slightly off his rocker,
The chap was definitely queer.
To make a single cap I wager
Would take, at least, one ursa major,
And that's an awful lot of bear.

To use the proper nomenclature,
A busby elongates the stature;
A midget towers in the air.
The headgear comes down to their noses
All they can see are their own toeses,
And those are not so very clear.

Moreover and finally

It covers all the cranium
And atrophies the brainium
For lack of oxygenium,

so there.

While all this parading and clicking of heels was going on, I was standing with my face glued to the metal uprights of the fence which enclosed the Palace, while the crowd was pressing in increasing numbers behind me. I enthusiastically snapped pictures in all directions and was very pleased with the results later on when I had them developed. One of my best shots showed three bars of the fence at very close range, and, in the distance, something that might have been the heel of a guard disappearing around a corner.

Another equally good one was taken of the troops on parade as they marched up in front of the Palace. It was a most impressive sight at the time and I was anxious to capture it for posterity. One half of the snap turned out beautifully clear. It showed a man wheeling a baby carriage also a close-up rear view of two women. Regrettably the half where the troops should have been was completely obliterated.

Although my photographic attempts might not have

been considered too successful by some, nevertheless, I managed to obtain a very excellent imprint of the fence uprights on my face and this remained in evidence for some time.

On our agenda for the day were Westminster Abbey and St. Paul's Cathedral, so that took up the greater part of the afternoon. After these tours were completed we discovered that we had 25 minutes free time so we threw in the British Museum for good measure and then called it a day.

CHAPTER V

The next day we set out for Scotland on foot – I mean, by train. Actually it seemed at the time that we were walking the entire distance but that, of course, is not true; we walked only half the way. I had heard of the Flying Scotsman but I am not sure whether we were on that train or not. However, judging by the speed both forward and lateral, I am quite certain that it was at least a near relative of his.

I was made painfully aware of the lateral thrust when I walked the entire length of the train three times, colliding with every second seat that I passed, and experiencing major encounters in the vestibules, from which I finally emerged a crushed and beaten creature.

I must explain the necessity for all this walking; we were simply trying to locate the dining car. Assuming that it was at the rear of the train we staggered hopefully in that direction, passing through miles of cars, until we were eventually brought to a halt by the baggage car.

Deciding that we were obviously headed in the wrong direction, we about-faced and resumed our collision course in reverse.

For some unaccountable reason, the train seemed to have lengthened out considerably. Nevertheless, though buffeted and battered, we steadfastly forged ahead only to find ourselves at last in another baggage car. This was too much. I was tired, hungry and bruised in all the prominent parts of my anatomy. I sat down upon a mound of baggage and shed a bitter tear.

While I was thus indulging in profound self pity and also forming part of the excess baggage, my husband was continuing his quest for the elusive dining car. It had to be somewhere. It is true that we might have enquired from the train personnel providing we had encountered any of them. But they were nowhere in sight; they were probably all in the dining car having their afternoon tea.

At last my husband returned with the information that we had been headed in the right direction the first time but that we should have continued right through the baggage car. That meant that we had to weave our perilous course back again the entire length of the train. The passengers were now beginning to look slightly alarmed and shrank into their seats as we lurched by. But again we pressed on through all the cars which we had traversed twice before and through a few extra ones, which I swear they must have added when they saw us coming; then through the baggage car, and, at last, we reached our ultimate goal, the dining car.

By this time I was in a state of extreme exhaustion, verging on coma and the others, my husband and friends, were not much better. The waiter, probably sensing an acute crisis, promptly rushed in with four large teapots of piping hot, strong tea and accompanying pitchers of hot water and milk. After three cups of this invigorating infusion, we felt like normal human beings again and were anxious to obtain a little solid nutriment to go along with the tea.

But our waiter had disappeared. In fact, we never saw him again. He probably felt that he had completed his life's work when he brought us the tea and he was now applying for his pension.

After a lengthy interval another waiter arrived, apparently with the intention of presenting our bill. We explained that the first waiter had brought us tea only, but had not taken our order; also that we wished to order high tea as we wanted something substantial to eat. For some reason or other high tea was not available although the people opposite were finishing off what seemed to be a very satisfactory meal. However, he brought us sandwiches and cakes and, at no extra charge, four more pots of tea, as to him the idea of cold tea was unthinkable.

So we made the best of it, ate what was put in front of us and drank tea until we were awash and our faces were turning dark brown from the tannic acid. We now had eight large teapots on the table as the first ones had not been removed. When a third waiter arrived to tally up our bill, he looked with amazement at what appeared to be the Boston Tea Party, so we were obliged to explain the whole situation to him. Eventually everything was settled to our mutual satisfaction and we returned to our compartment.

Our destination was Lanark, where we were to stay with friends of our friends for a day or so. We had been advised to leave the train at Motherwell which was not too far from Lanark.

The guard on the train instructed us to carry our

luggage down next to the baggage car, otherwise on stepping off we would find ourselves a considerable distance from the platform. As it appeared that we were expected to carry it ourselves, away we went again along the old familiar route, but this time burdened with everything that we possessed.

Our progress was nothing short of lethal, that is to the passengers who cringed in their seats and uttered weak protests as they were jabbed indiscriminately with the edges of suitcases, umbrellas, and bags.

When I looked back at my husband trying to cope with two heavy bags I was startled to note that his arms had stretched about six inches and were now reaching below his knees. Even his jaws had a definitely prognathous look due to the expression of grim determination on his face. This reversion to type or devolution to a Neanderthal man can be very disconcerting to watch, especially when it happens to one's own husband.

As we waited in the entry we were joined by two gentlemen who evidently had been celebrating their return to the land of the heather. They were, in maritime vernacular, three sheets in the wind. When they learned that we were from Nova Scotia and were intent on visiting the country of our forefathers, they were so overwhelmed by the wonder of it all that they were reduced to tears. But, fortunately, before things became too maudlin, the train pulled in at Motherwell. It was with difficulty that we dissuaded our new found friends from helping us with our luggage. It was obvious that, short of falling off, they would have considerable difficulty getting themselves off the train.

In spite of everything we all managed somehow without mishap and in a short time we were travelling towards Lanark where we spent several delightful days.

As this was my first meeting with any Lowland Scottish people, I found myself at times puzzled by some of their expressions or phrases as well as by their accent, and, no doubt, this was reciprocal. For example, that first evening when our hostess turned to me and said quite matter-of-factly "Your Mac is in the boot" I was completely at a loss. When she saw that she was not getting through, she repeated it a little louder thinking that I was a trifle hard of hearing. Not wishing to appear too stupid, I tried to assume what I imagined was a reasonably intelligent expression but behind that outer façade of brain power my mind was a blank.

Nevertheless I tried to come up with translation that might be acceptable. Perhaps she was referring to my husband as 'Mac' since he was a MacKay and 'boot' might be a slang term for jail. As he had gone out earlier in the evening to look the town over, the possibility of his landing in jail was not too remote.

But she did not seem to be unduly concerned, so I decided that I, too, would be nonchalant. After all, what is one more jail term anyway? It seemed that I was expected to say or do something but I adroitly side-stepped the issue by muttering a few incoherent words. She, naturally, was unable to interpret them but that was to be expected as I, myself, did not know what I was saying.

Days later, when I became more conversant with the British way of speaking, it dawned upon me that she had been merely telling me that my raincoat had been left in the trunk of her car.

Other words which were at some variance with our

own were the terms for meals: *Lunch* applied only to the noon-time repast. Any snack or, as we would say 'lunch', served before bedtime was a *supper*. What we call supper was their *high tea*. Dinner was served around 7 or 8 p.m. and in case you couldn't survive through the day there was coffee at mid-morning and afternoon tea around 4 p.m.

CHAPTER VI

Edinburgh was our objective for the next day and our hostess most obligingly took a day off from her own activities and motored us there.

As we approached the capital, the weather which had been rather misty when we left Lanark, became increasingly drippy. As we entered Princes Street our attention was called to Edinburgh Castle on our right, but it was just a shadowy and sinister mass seen through wraithlike tendrils of fog. At any rate, fog or not, it seemed as good a place as any to start our explorations. As we reached the Castle the sense of the macabre increased rather than lessened. It was a beautiful spot, that is for a murder; but as no willing victim was available I was filled with an inordinate sense of loss. To have a perfect setting for a crime and no crime to commit is sheer frustration. Psychiatrists would probably tell you that this might leave you scarred for life.

In spite of the weather we went up and down the Royal Mile, which is on the Castle eminence and a famous part of the Old Town. The new town of Edinburgh came into being in 1767. We were shown St. Giles Cathedral which is of Norman architecture.

The stone was brought over from Iona around the twelth century.

Within this cathedral there is a Thistle Chapel reserved for the Knights of the Thistle. The Geddes Entry is a side chapel reserved for any denomination. We would have liked to have seen the interior of this famous church but for some reason or other we were debarred. I was aware that we might find it difficult to pass ourselves off as Knights of the Thistle as it is a very exclusive order, having only 18 members at present, and the unheralded influx of four or five new members might prove a trifle embarrassing to them.

I would have been willing to settle for the lowlier Geddes entry but that too was closed, so we contented ourselves with admiring from the outside the angels playing the bagpipes over the doorway.

There were many things of interest to observe along the Royal Mile and in the vicinity. We were shown the house where Daniel Defoe had lived, the Canongate Tolbooth Museum, the Blue Blanket, a restored pub, the World's End Close and various other 'Closes'.

When I first heard the word 'Close' mentioned it was in reference to the Lyon's Close. We were told that this particular narrow entrance or alley-like passage led to property of the Lyon's family, the family of the present Queen Mother. As I was under the impression they were talking about 'clothes', I peered through the entrance expecting to see the Monday wash waving in the breeze.

But it was time for a coffee break so we abandoned the Castle and its surroundings to their own gloomy reminiscences and wandered down towards Princes Street.

Before long we found ourselves in front of Sir Walter Scott's Memorial. This is a very imposing structure and it would have been better if we had remained outside and admired it from a distance. But at the entrance there was a guard selling tickets for 1s 6d each which permitted one to enter therein, presumably to see something. Now if there had been no entrance fee we probably would not have bothered going inside at all, but since we had to pay we concluded that this was something we had waited all our lives to see.

That conclusion is, of course, a *non sequitur,* but as most of us would not recognize a *non sequitur* if we fell over it, we blithely paid our money and went in. We were immediately confronted by a spiral staircase, which was strictly on the up-and-up. So up we went on a corkscrew course. The higher we mounted, the narrower the stairway and the more numerous the spirals.

It soon became disturbingly evident that while the head and shoulders were negotiating a new convolution, the lower extremities were still plodding along in the opposite direction in an effort to complete the previous spiral. The effect of all this stress and strain on the human torso would have to be experienced in order to be appreciated.

Breathing was difficult due to the rarefied atmosphere. There were 287 steps as I found out later but my muscles and lungs gave out about the 199th step, so I emerged on a platform and looked around. But there was nothing to see but fog and mist so I spiralled my way down, automatically unwinding myself in the reverse process. I understand that anyone who completes the entire ascent is given some

View of interior of Scott's Monument showing spiral stairs partly obscured by cloud.

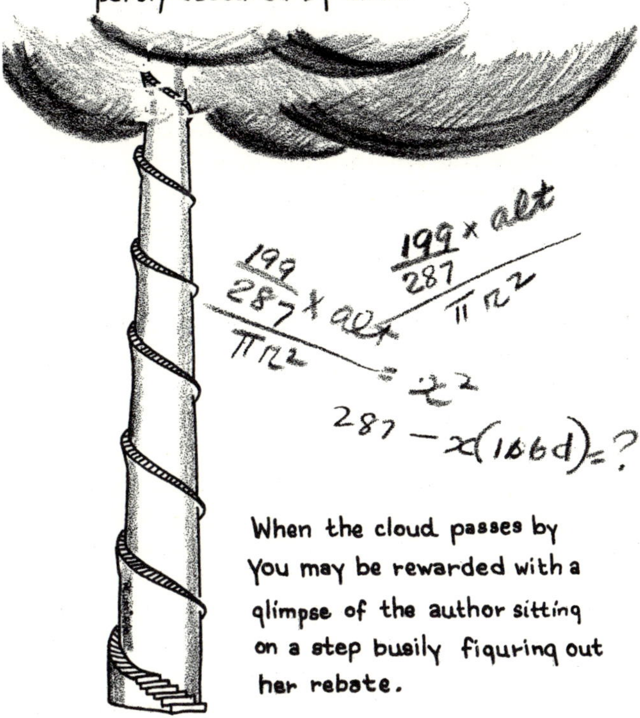

When the cloud passes by you may be rewarded with a glimpse of the author sitting on a step busily figuring out her rebate.

sort of award, probably a crown of glory for so nearly approaching Heaven.

But for myself, I was considering the idea of requesting a rebate on my ticket worked out on a *pro rata* basis, namely 199/287ths of 1s 6d. So I sat myself down on the lowest step and proceeded to engage in some intricate computations.

An hour later I had come up with three possible answers, all carefully checked, re-checked and verified. I liked best the one where I would be refunded £1 3s 2d but I was doubtful whether the man at the wicket would see it my way. In the meantime I was obstructing traffic so in deference to Mr Scott I decided it would be best to let the whole matter drop.

The following day, as the weather was somewhat improved, we were better able to appreciate Edinburgh. The day's activities included a visit to the Palace of Holyrood. Near the Palace are the ruins of Holyrood Abbey which was built by David I and completed in 1128. The Palace dates from the sixteenth century and is used at present on State occasions.

Any castle or palace would be considered incomplete without its quota of murders, and this particular place was no exception. A bronze tablet inserted in the floor marks the spot where the body of David Rizzio was left after his murder in the supper room of Mary Queen of Scots. As all the gory details were related with gusto by the guide, we all enjoyed a shudderingly good time.

The Art Gallery somewhere in the vicinity provided a pleasant and educational interlude. I love art galleries; there are so many places to sit down. Years ago I decided that the best way to get an appreciation of the great masterpieces was to sit in front of one for a considerable length of time, until one had achieved a semi-comatose state or until one was ejected by the guard at closing time. If a brief siesta could be managed, so much the better; the process of absorbing culture is then taken over by one's sub-conscious, thus eliminating a lot of wear and tear on the cerebrum. It is astounding how much culture I have acquired by this method over the course of years.

Later on we paused to admire and pass the time of day with the floral clock at one of the entrances to the park. This is a masterpiece of precision planting; even the hands say it accurately with flowers. I was determined to get a snap of it and, for once, to my complete surprise I was rewarded with an excellent picture. The inscription on the face of the clock shows 'Investiture 1969'. What surprised me most was that the inscription came out right side up as, in order to take it, I was forced to literally hang by my feet with my back to the clock and hold the camera over my left shoulder. As I had been prepared to see it emerge as 'erutitsevni 6961', the result was all the more gratifying.

That evening as I stood on Princes Street with the rain trickling down my neck while I waited for a bus, I was enthralled by the picture in front of me. The Castle was directly opposite on its craggy heights with the floodlights playing on it and beneath it was the beautiful setting of the Gardens; it seemed like an enchanted city and I was loath to leave it. So after a little consultation with my husband, we decided to remain in Edinburgh for a week or so while making it our headquarters for tours.

Our friends returned to Lanark but promised to

rejoin us later on in Glasgow, where we had booked a 7 day tour to Strathpeffer.

We had the address of a private rooming house run by a Mrs Gordon and were fortunate to be able to make reservations there for the following week. We were given a very pleasant, comfortable room and Mrs Gordon proved to be a delightful person who did everything in her power to make our stay a happy one.

The following day we took a bus tour of the City and so many interesting things were pointed out that it is difficult to recall them all. To mention just a few of them, there was St. Mary's Anglican Cathedral, donated by two sisters; the house where Scott wrote the Waverley Novels; a number of buildings built by the Adams Brothers; these structures are not allowed to be altered or defaced. We also saw the birthplace of Alexander Graham Bell. I might add that I have seen many times the place where he is buried. It is on the top of a hill called Beinn Bhreagh and commands a beautiful view of the Bras D'Or Lakes in Cape Breton Island. A huge uncut boulder, with a simple inscription on it and the dates 1847 - 1922, marks his grave.

On one pleasantly warm day we went out to the Royal Botanic Gardens and Arboretum. In one of the hot-houses, devoted to tropical plants only I was greatly impressed by what seemed to be a species of water lily. They looked like huge, shallow, circular pans floating on the surface of the water, some of them almost a yard in width, green on the inside and shrimp color without. I took several snaps and again was surprised by my ever increasing expertise, as they turned out beautifully.

Underneath these hothouses were aquariums, where

you could view from underneath what you had already seen right side up on the surface.

One very nice thing about Edinburgh is that a park extends all along one side of Princes Street, which is the main commercial thoroughfare, so that if one gets tired of shopping it is easy to cross over and rest awhile. An intriguing aspect of this park is that a railway goes through it but one is not even aware of it, even though the tracks are on the surface. It is so ingeniously camouflaged with shrubbery that trains, which are constantly passing through it *en route* to nearby Waverley Station, achieve almost total invisibility. A slight rumbling may be heard at times, which, when I first heard it, I attributed to some Scotsman up on Princes Street grumbling about the high price of haggis.

After obtaining some slight idea of Edinburgh we decided to branch out a bit to the surrounding country. Perhaps a few general remarks about my impressions and observations derived from my tours around the country might be appropriate just now. I shall put all this heterogeneous information under the scholarly heading of

Errata et Inaccurata

One of the first of the many surprising things I learned about Scotland was that it had only one lake. From this one might deduce, but quite erroneously, that the country was an arid wasteland. But such is not the case; the ingenuity of the Scotsman has again come to the fore and he has devised innumerable lochs, separated here and there by bens to prevent the lochs from flowing into one another.

At first glance one might assume that a loch was identical with a lake but closer study would reveal essential differences. In the first place a loch is more guttural. Then again its deep and brooding personality differs from the light-hearted approach to living shown by a lake. One does not treat a loch lightly; they harbor at times, huge eels, as big around as a man's thigh, so it is said, and things or persons that are unfortunate enough to fall into a loch are seldom seen or heard of again. And then there are monsters in their depths, but I will devote more time to that later.

There is only one criticism I might make while on the subject of lochs and it is this: even though lochs are undoubtedly terrifically scenic and without them Scotland might prove quite ordinary, nevertheless the Scots went a little overboard, they were over zealous in their distribution of lochs; they have them all over the place and they come in all kinds and sizes; you can have a fresh or salt water loch; where there is not sufficient room for a large one then they put in a small one, which they call a lochan.

The bens, as was intimated in a previous paragraph. have an essential and practical function but they also have other uses, such as being places to put sheep, deer, mountain climbers, reindeer, grouse, and skiers. They also provide the Government with more surface area for the planting of trees.

The Forestry Commission seems to have an inordinate fondness for this sort of activity and, to date, has about 800,000 acres planted in trees. Practically all of these plantings are softwood, spruce, pine, larches and some Douglas fir from British Columbia. Personally I would like to see more hardwood trees, interspersed for variety in form and color, with the evergreen trees; also not quite such a regimental style of planting.

But, apparently, when a Scotsman undertakes anything he is a dedicated man; nothing will deter him from his appointed task. He will deviate neither to right nor left. So if trees are to be planted, he will plant them by the millions and this is literally true. I read where back between the years 1775 and 1825 "John the 4th Duke of Atholl, is reputed to have planted over 14 million trees. In inaccessible places he fired bags of seed from a cannon."*

The planted areas are carefully enclosed with high wire fences in order to prevent the entrance of any wild life. It is doubtful whether Bobbie Burns' tim'rous beastie would be granted asylum in any of these sterile forests.

As the planting of trees continues and, I understand, the quota of 50,000 trees a year is set by the Forestry Commission, the amount of sheep grazing land is diminished and consequently the number of sheep. Thus the forests will take over again and the cycle will have started anew.

I will itemize briefly in chronological order the series of events which have taken place:

1. Trees – huge Caledonian forests
2. Humans, including Highlanders
3. Trees destroyed
4. Highlanders shoved off cliffs of north-west Scotland, some making it to Canada
5. Sheep introduced in their place – more profitable than Highlanders but not so good in battle

*Article by Alastair Campbell in *Scots Magazine*, September, 1969.

6. Sheep now being reduced to make way for trees
7. Reindeer brought in to take over higher mountain peaks where even trees won't grow
8. Back to trees again

When they get around to Highlanders once again and are looking to Canada to supply them I doubt whether the response will be overwhelming. It is not good to tamper with the ecology of a land. There should be a happy diversity of plants, humans and other animal life with tolerance towards all. Besides, what are they going to do with all the cones off the conifers – make Christmas decorations?

Talking about sheep, even though their number *is* diminishing, you still see them everywhere. There are a number of varieties, but I noted particularly one type, which I was told, were "white-faced Cheviots". These are specially adapted to thrive under the severe climatic conditions of northern Scotland. The story goes that when the first sheep to arrive looked around them and viewed the rocky terrain on which they were supposed to subsist, and on which their predecessors, the Highlanders, had existed for years, they turned white in the face and never quite got over it.

But the sheep are not all white or black or variations of these colors. At one place I actually saw brilliant orange colored sheep; what they were trying to prove, by their spectacular deviation from the norm, I do not know.

I have discussed lochs and bens; there are other things in a like category but I shall only mention them briefly, as they have no particular practical use, other than to confuse the tourist. They are: straths, kyles, firths, sounds and mulls, etc. Should you come across any of these it is best to ignore them. With regard to rivers, I have made an intensive study of the subject, the results of which I shall present later on.

* * * * * * *

As the tourist season was practically over we found that quite a few of the bus tours had been discontinued and we were limited in our choice. However, we were able to book a day tour to Aberdeen and several other afternoon tours.

Our Aberdeen tour took us northward and along the eastern shore-line. First we went over the Forth Bridge which was completed in 1964. It is 512 feet high or long, I am not sure which, not being good at statistics. At any rate it is looked upon as something special. Fortunately it is quite functional, so we journeyed forth over the Firth of Forth with forthitude. (Sorry about that). The railway bridge which is parallel to it was built in 1890.

I shall mention only a few of the many places that we passed through; there was Cowdenbeath, which is a mining town, and then Auchtermuchty, and next Dundee, which is situated on the northern shore of the Firth of Tay.

Our first stop was at Arbroath, where we had our morning coffee. This town is on the eastern coast facing the North Sea. It is noted for Arbroath Abbey which dates from 1233. Here the monks of Kelso drew up the famous Declaration of Independence in 1320 making Scotland a free country.

Scone, which is in the vicinity, is the site of the ancient palace where so many Scottish kings were crowned and where the Stone of Scone reposed for years. The origin of this cracked stone seems to be disputed; some say that it was a Pictish stone taken from Dunstaffnage Castle near Oban; others say that it originally came from Tara in Ireland. Whatever its origin, it was used for years to crown kings with, this probably accounting for its crack. It finally came to rest in 1293 in Westminster Abbey, where, with the exception of a brief unscheduled return visit to its homeland, it has remained to this day.

The trouble with Scotland is that it has too much history. One can't go anywhere without having to clutter up one's mind with dates and historical facts. A certain amount of this is necessary but the greater part could well be eliminated. You know, a little history goes a long way.

Over in Nova Scotia, where we have only a little over 200 years to account for, we still can get awfully mixed up even on that. History has a habit of going in cycles. For instance, in Cape Breton the French built this fortress at Louisbourg; then the English came along and captured it but they gave it back to the French as it was the best two out of three that counted; so they had another go at it and captured it again. This time, as the game was over, they demolished it completely, including the King's Bastion and all the dishes. That was back in 1748 or was it 1758 or both?

Today it is being all put back again exactly the way it was in the first place; the bastions are up once more and the dishes have all been dug up and stuck together with glue. I expect they want to have some history to show the tourists when they come around or perhaps they are merely getting it ready for a third capture, sort of standing it up in order to knock it down.

If you will pardon my digression, we shall return to our tour. After Arbroath we saw a succession of small coastal villages such as Gordon, Inverbervie and Stonehaven, which is a thriving little port and county town with a very picturesque harbour.

We had a disappointingly short stay at Aberdeen with just time enough for lunch. We learned a few facts, however, from our courier, namely that Aberdeen is called the Granite City and that St. Andrew's University is the second largest granite building in the world, the largest being in Spain.

From Aberdeen we turned west and inland to Balmoral, a distance of about 50 miles, first passing through Banchory, where we stopped to visit the Dee Lavender Plant, and then on through Ballater, which is a holiday resort.

It was while in this section of this country that I first noticed brooms placed at irregular intervals along the side of the road. Later on I saw them in several other places but I never did find out why they were there. They looked like what we used to call 'birch broom' made out of reeds tied around a handle of the type used by witches. I can only conclude that they were left there either by the witches or for the witches. As Hallowe'en was not too far off preparations were probably being made well in advance for their nocturnal air flights.

Our bus stopped in front of the Church near Balmoral Castle. This is the church where the Royal family worship. We walked over towards the Castle but did not get beyond the gate as the Queen was in residence at the time. This is where that blueberry pie might have given me an entrée to the Castle. I doubt whether even royalty could resist a luscious pie filled with blueberries fresh picked from the hills of Nova Scotia.

Then on to Braemar, where we were served a delicious afternoon tea at the Fyfe Arms Hotel. Then by way of the Devil's Elbow, a series of very steep turns which our bus driver was forced to negotiate very slowly. This gave him time to tell us the story of the Scotsman who was touring in Ireland. As he passed a certain point he was told that it was the Devil's Elbow. The Scot replied "It can't be, because the Devil's Elbow is in Scotland." This did not phase the Irishman for he promptly returned: "Sure, but the devil has two elbows."

Our return journey took us through Blairgowrie and Perth and from there back to Edinburgh by the same route that we had come.

Another afternoon we took a very interesting tour southward through Midlothian country with the Pentland Hills on our right. We passed through the town of Penicuik, which is a paper making town; it is here that the first treasury notes in the country were made; next through the Village of Romano Bridge which, as the name suggests, was first settled by the Romans. We continued to the heart of the Moorfoot Hills, where three rivers have their source: the Tweed, which flows 103 miles into the North Sea, the Clyde flowing westerly, and the Annan flowing south.

In a short time we arrived at the Devil's Beef Tub, but there was nothing cooking at the moment. It is, indeed, a quite remarkable sight. From our vantage point on the highway we could look down into a sort of chasm, more or less bowl shaped and 1300 feet in depth. Most days, we were told, it is partly filled with mist which conveys the idea of a boiling cauldron. But on this particular day it was clear and we could see what was called a 'fairy ring' at the bottom. This is in reality an enclosure made from rocks which offers some sort of shelter for sheep.

Our journey then took us through the lovely Annadale Valley, until we reached the town of Moffatt where we stopped for our afternoon tea. We also took the opportunity to visit the Moffatt Weavers Shop which specialized in tartans, etc. Presumably weaving is a prime industry in this section of the country as we noticed in the Square a monument of a ram.

From Moffatt we returned by a different route, passing by the Grey Mare's Tail Falls. These flow from Loch Skene, a very narrow stream of water falling 300 feet. Our course took us past the village of Traquair, dating from the twelfth century, then through the villages of Interleith and Peebles and back to Edinburgh.

The following morning we left this lovely city regretfully but we were anxious to see more of northern Scotland. So we went by train to Inverness, where we remained for a few days, taking whatever tours were available at the time. The first trip that we took out of Inverness was an afternoon tour to Aviemore and the Cairngorms. Our route followed in a southerly direction through the villages of Daviot and Moy; then through the village of Tomatin which is situated near the River Findhorn. This river is about 60 miles long and flows into the North Sea; then through Slochd Summit which is 1315 feet above sea level (should anyone be interested) and then the town of Carrbridge.

It was at this point that the bus stopped long enough for us to take a snap of a very picturesque foot bridge which we were told was built originally to enable the dead to get across to the other side. Why they should want to get across, I don't know, as one side seemed much the same as the other. Perhaps this stream was considered something in the nature of the River Styx.

At Coylumbridge we turned left to the Cairngorms. This is a vast mountain range which was formed by placing a number of bens in juxtaposition. As only the highest of the bens were used in this project, all being over 4,000 feet, the resulting range is the highest in Great Britain.

Our coach obligingly took us part-way up the mountain to a height of 2,000 feet where we stopped at a ski lodge and restaurant in what, I believe, is called Coire Cas Car Park. If one were venturesome and could withstand the process of quick freezing, one could take the chair lifts which rose in two sections to a height of 4,000 feet, affording magnificent views of the countryside, if one could be thawed out sufficiently to enjoy them.

Shortly after we left the Lodge we saw several reindeer in an enclosure. We were told that this was sort of a reindeer hospital and these two were convalescing. I guess that even reindeer find it hard to cope with the Cairngorms.

Aviemore is a very modern resort in the heart of this ski country. There are chalets, hotels, a modern shopping mall, ice skating rinks, curling rinks, swimming pools and everything else necessary for a vacation resort. After a nice afternoon tea at one of the hotels, we returned by the same route to Inverness.

One of our more interesting trips was an all day tour to Durness and north-west Sutherland. Leaving

Inverness we crossed the river Ness. This river is only 6 miles long but makes up for its lack of length by having a very swift current. It is the only river flowing out of Loch Ness although there are seven rivers flowing in. We did not see the Loch at this time but did later on.

On this occasion we travelled along Beauly Firth, with the Black Isle opposite, then along to Dingwall, the county town of Ross and Cromarty, dating from 1226, and then along to Aultnamain. It was in this area that we noticed quite a number of people cutting peat. It seems that in a lot of sections they are going back to peat for fuel, as coal has become too expensive.

When we reached Ardgay we stopped for morning coffee. It was developing into a lovely day; the weather had not been too good since our arrival in Inverness, mostly strong gales and rain, so we were all the more appreciative of this sunny, warm day.

At Lairg the sheep sales were in progress and we saw hundreds of sheep in pens, and as we went along we passed many three-tiered trucks, carrying as many as 300 sheep at one time. We were told that buyers came from all over Scotland and northern England. Lairg is the real head of all north-west Scotland. It is situated on Loch Shin which is about 18 miles in length. For awhile the terrain was mostly peaty marsh-lands and hills, very poor looking land and there were no homes in sight; even the sheep had deserted it, but we were informed that we would soon be getting into good deer country and, sure enough, we spotted a dozen or more on the distant hills. When they are standing still they are almost invisible against the background of bronze coloured broom and heather;

it is only when they move that they become noticeable.

We continued past Loch Laxford and Loch Inchard and in a short time arrived at Rhiconich where we stopped to enjoy a very good lunch. Leaving there we traversed a rocky, bleak country with no people, no sheep and no deer in evidence until we approached Durness. At Durness we were on the northern coast of Scotland, almost as far north as John O'Groats and facing the Atlantic Ocean. From here we could see the lighthouse of Cape Wrath in the distance. At that cape there was a honeycomb of underground shelters during the war.

Our bus stopped long enough for us to view the entrance to the Smoo Cave, which is on the ocean side of the road. This is a large, menacing, Stygian cave with a turbulent stream flowing through it. I would not want to explore its depths even if that were possible. I wondered how it got its name. Suddenly, while I was ruminating about it, the answer came to me like a flash. It obviously was the habitat of a smoo. So I sat down on a convenient rock and penned the following impression of a smoo.

LINES
WRITTEN AT THE ENTRANCE TO SMOO CAVE

A genuine authentic smoo
Is seldom seen outside a zoo,
And never seen inside one;
Yet some returning home at morn
From partying with John Barleycorn
Have sworn that they have spied one.

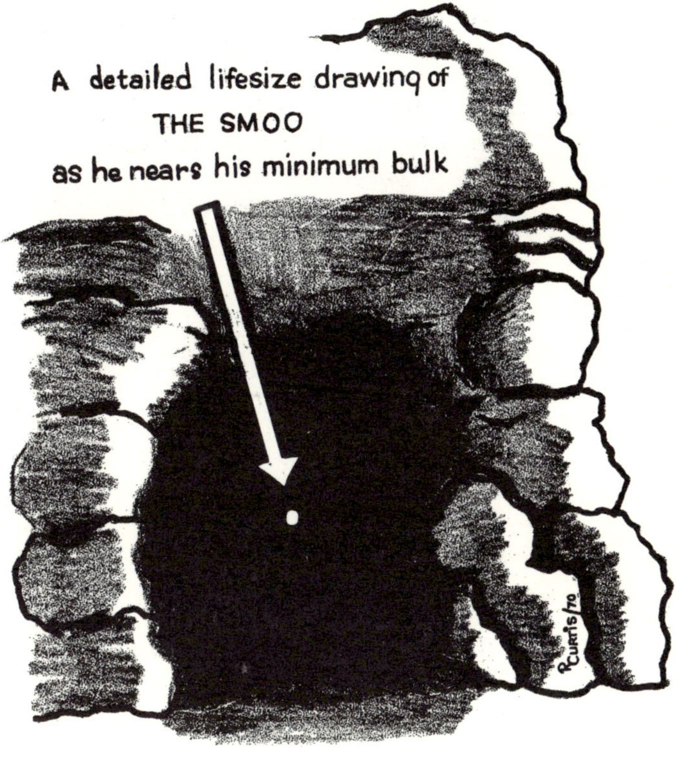

"At times he's hardly there
at all."

It's claimed that he's a vertebrate
While others, with conviction, state
He's sort of jelly-fishy;
The truth is that, at times, he's one
And then the other, just for fun;
He's slightly washy-wishy.

You'll see him best at crack of dawn,
He rushes here and there and yon
And to and fro and thither;
He's out to get the early bird
That got the worm that early stirred;
He raises quite a dither.

The smoo is neither fish nor fowl,
At times he's hardly there at all
But then, to be contrary,
His chest expands, his eyes dilate
He grows to a gigantic height,
He's positively scary.

At times his mental faculties
Surpass those of the chimpanzees,
Displaying great acumen;
At other times he's very dense
In fact he makes so little sense
He's practically human.

After we left the home of the schizophrenic smoo, we had a lovely drive along the coast with its many sandy beaches. We stopped to view one marvellous beach which seemed perfectly symmetrical and looked wonderful for swimming. I would have liked to have gone down and tried the water, which might not have been too cold even for late September, as the Gulf stream swings around that northern coast moderating the temperatures.

Then on around Loch Eriboll. From here we could see Ben Hope, which is 3,000 feet high and Ben Loyal (Ben Laoghal was the old Gaelic name). At Loch Hope, which is a fresh water loch, we passed a very modern looking fishing lodge. Then we went on to the Kyle of Tongue and the village of Tongue, which is situated in what seems to be fairly good farming country.

After that the road became very narrow and in one instance the bus was forced to back up a considerable distance in order to let a truck pass. In most of these northern highlands and in the western islands such as Mull the roads are made for one lane traffic only but they have what they call 'lay-bys' at frequent intervals to facilitate passing. If there is no lay-by handy when two vehicles approach from opposite directions, then it is the survival of the fittest and the weaker one retreats to the nearest lay-by.

But the roads, even though narrow, were uniformly good, and as nobody was in any particular hurry, such incidents and delays only added a little interest to the journey. Actually some of these roads I mentioned might be classified as belonging to the two-lane variety, that is, there are two parallel concrete strips, a car's width apart, leaving a grassy strip in the centre. At first, I thought that this was the Scottish way of economizing in the construction of roads, but later on was told that the strip in the centre was left so that it would prevent the horses from slipping in the winter time.

When we had first arrived in London we had toyed

with the notion of renting a car and driving ourselves around the country but we abandoned the idea when we noticed that everyone drove on the wrong side of the road. That, I believe, is an excellent example of how an error can be perpetuated and proliferated until it is generally accepted as right. The first chap to drive a car in the British Isles probably did not know his right hand from his left, and thus the error arose and continues to this day. We were therefore glad to let our driver cope with these problems and he did it most efficiently in spite of the error of his ways.

But again I digress; I think that it was near Tongue that the ruins of an ancient Pictish castle were seen, mouldering away on its rocky eminence. We started back on our return trip by way of Altnaharra and then back to Lairg. From then on we followed much the same route, except for a detour to Tain and Invergordon, that we had covered in the morning.

Tain dates back to 1066 and celebrated its ninth centenary in 1966. The Queen Mother was present for the occasion and had 900 rose bushes planted in the public gardens there.

Invergordon was an important place during wartime as the fleet was stationed there. Now it is no longer a naval station, but new industries of aluminum and oil have been established and are expected to do a great deal for the economy.

Before leaving Inverness we visited the Museum and Art Gallery, a modern complex including cocktail lounge and library. We also viewed the Castle of the Duncans where King Duncan was buried in 1040. His death probably occurred around that date too.

I had hoped to visit the Culloden Moor Battlefield, which is only a short distance from Inverness, but my husband did not seem at all enthusiastic about the idea. When I pressed him for his reason for not wanting to go, he replied that he had been on a battlefield ever since he got married and that was enough.

Oban was our next objective, the land of the McDougalls of Lorne. So we left Inverness by bus, travelling in a south-west direction along the Caledonian Canal, with stops at Fort Augustus and Fort William and crossing on a small ferry at Ballachulish.

Oban greeted us with a dazzling array of flowers, still wonderfully fresh for the time of year, displayed in a small park at the entrance to the town. Our hotel at Oban was a pleasant one on the Esplanade and it provided an excellent view of the water front with the mountains of Mull and Morven across the harbour in the distance.

Oban impressed us at once as being much more than a tourist resort, although the Esplanade is lined with hotels, some of them quite luxurious. But the life of a small, active town goes on around you; it was interesting to walk to the docks and see the fishing boats at anchor or coming in the harbour; it was quite common to see seals in the harbour and there were birds of all sorts to hold one's attention.

On one occasion we saw about 100 sheep or more being landed on the dock perhaps brought down from Skye. They were shepherded by a drover with the help of three sheep dogs. The drover was a tall, rangy fellow wearing a woollen cap pulled well down on his head and he seemed the personification of a highlander in action.

As he called out orders to the dogs, the head one took his place at the head of the flock and proceeded to lead them, while the other two dogs went on either side to keep the sheep from straying. Now this was a busy dock and a busy time of day. The area was filled with people coming off the excursion boats and cars were coming and going, but the head dog ignored them all. He had a job to do and he did it. As he obeyed the shouted instructions of the drover the cars and people had to make way for him, and so he led the flock off the dock and away.

After we got settled a bit we followed our usual procedure and found out what tours were available. We were fortunate to be able to make reservations for four of them, which would keep us pretty well occupied for our stay.

Our first tour was an afternoon trip to Easdale. This is a picturesque fishing village on the coast of the Firth of Lorne. As we passed Loch Feochan we could see, over on the opposite side, Dunoch House with its 365 windows. What a problem the housewife would have trying to keep them all supplied with curtains and drapes. Perhaps the owners merely wanted to make sure that they would not miss anything going on at the Loch and would have a clear view of proceedings. For on this same loch 48, presumably dead, Scottish kings were taken to Iona for burial. In confirmation of their deaths, there are stones standing today in the centre of the loch and they are called Stones of the Dead. So from those 365 windows could be seen quite a lot of pageantry in years gone by.

At Clachan Bridge, the bridge over the Atlantic, we crossed to the Island of Seil. I think that it was here that we were shown the hotel known as the 'House of the Trousers'. This name dates back to the time when the

Easdale, near Oban

highlanders stopped here to remove their trousers and don their kilts, or *vice versa,* depending on whether they were going or coming from whatever they were doing.

There was a tea-room at Easdale but for once we did without our afternoon tea and wandered around a novelty shop which we found most interesting. The owner of the shop was an artist and his paintings adorned both walls and ceilings. Moreover, there was Scottish music and we were treated with homemade fudge.

Quarrying had been at one time the main industry at Easdale but in 1881 the state quarries were flooded and abandoned. It has been superseded now by forestry and road work.

By way of variation we had arranged for a few boat cruises or a combination of coach and boat tours. Accordingly the next day we left for a tour of the islands of Mull and Iona. As we came out of Oban Harbour and skirted the shore we had a good view of Dunollie Castle, which is the seat of the McDougall Clan.

As this is my clan I felt that it was only right and proper that I should have a picture of this castle. So politely edging myself in between some people standing at the rail of the ship, I said: "Pardon me, but I must take a picture of my ancestral castle." They looked a bit startled and even a trifle deferential, or so I imagined, but they moved aside and I obtained my picture.

After docking at Craignure on Mull we joined our coach for a tour of the island. We stopped at Pennyghael on the shores of Loch Scridain for lunch, then on to Fionphort where we crossed by a small ferry to Iona. My chief recollection of the crossing was the remarkable crystal clearness of the water.

It was in the year 563 they tell us that "St. Columba stepped from his Irish coracle to the shores of Iona and set about converting Scotland to Christianity." Why he picked Iona is hard to see, as the island appears to be rocky and almost barren. There are so many more prepossessing islands scattered all around. The fact that there were abundant supplies of granite in the neighbourhood might have been a deciding factor for he and his monks had to build an abbey, and even a saint has to be practical.

The Abbey was erected in that same year. Although it was later destroyed it was rebuilt in 1500 and the ruins of that later Abbey were restored 1902-12 by the Church of Scotland. It is said that there are 60 kings buried there. In addition to the 48 Scottish ones, the last of whom was Macbeth, who, as I mentioned, left the mainland at Loch Feochan, there were eight Norwegian and four Irish kings. The paved cobblestone road over which the remains were borne was unearthed not so many years ago and is called the 'Street of the Dead'.

As we left Iona I had the feeling that we had just seen the stage on which a tremendous drama had been enacted and that the curtain had been rung down for the last time.

On our return journey through Mull we noticed Ben More, which rises to a height of 3,169 feet and is the highest point on the island. It is an extinct volcano and the molten lava which poured out from its crater eons ago can still be seen in places. When the sun hits it in a certain direction it gleams like a waterfall on the side of the mountain. No vegetation

Iona Ferry

can grow on it even after centuries.

The village of Bunessan on the peninsula of the Ross of Mull is noted for its granite quarries and pink granite is seen everywhere.

I was becoming a little tired of all those lochs; not that I had anything against them *per se* as they were all very lovely; but they were ubiquitous which is the worst thing I could say about them. My mind was beginning to rebel in its effort to sort them all out as to which was which and where. So I said to myself and to anyone who would listen: "No more lochs".

This resolution held only until the following morning when our itinerary showed that we were scheduled to take a whole day circular cruise. This is called the Cruise to the Six Lochs and the Corrievrekan Whirlpool. So away we went again. According to the map of the route we were supposed to sail in a clockwise direction but the Captain must have got a bit mixed up for he sailed counter-clockwisely. This mixed us all up until we got wise to what was going on.

I am not going even to list the names of the lochs that we called on that day. Whenever I felt one coming on I retired to the lounge and curled up with a good book. However, I did notice some islands. On Lismore Island can be seen the ruins of Achinduin Castle (the Bishop's Palace) also the ruins of Castle Rachael, an ancient Scandinavian Fortress.

As we cruised down the Firth of Lorne we passed on our right Garvelloch Isles or Holy Isles. There is an ancient burial ground, church and monastery at one end of these isles. Some histories say that this was the first landing place of Saint Columba.

When we reached the island of Scarba we turned easterly and went through the strait of Corrievrekan between the islands of Scarba and Jura. This was supposed to be the locale of the big whirlpool, but he was not whirling that day – apparently had the day off. The water was quite turbulent nevertheless, and there were any number of minor whirlpools disporting themselves here and there.

On our homeward course as we approached the island of Kerrara, which is just off Oban, we could see Gylen Castle, which at one time was also a stronghold of the MacDougalls. It was besieged and captured by General Leslie in 1647. It was getting too dark to take any snap of it, so we returned to Oban after quite a day on the water.

The following day we made Inverary our objective. The outward journey was partly over the same route we had traversed on our trip to Easdale. As we went through Kilmore village the smallest post-office in the world was pointed out to us. It looked to be about 6′ x 6′ or less. It would not do to mail any long envelopes in that place.

Then on to Kilmartin where we stopped at an attractive small hotel for morning coffee. Kilmartin has an amazing history for there is evidence of occupation there dating back to 3,000 B.C. or earlier. At a time when the Egyptians were busy building their pyramids, the Stone Age men were erecting their cairns at Kilmartin. One of them (I refer to the cairns, not the men) can be seen today about a mile south of the village. It is said that it is easy to enter and stand within the burial chamber which has withstood the storms of nearly 50 centuries.

Many cairns may be seen in the fields surrounding

the village, some dating from the Bronze Age. Then along the road a different sort of ancient burial site may be seen. It is known as the Temple Wood Stone Circle. Here there is a large central cist standing in a circle of erect stones. This dates from about 2,000 B.C.

If any place deserves to be haunted then Kilmartin is that place. One could take ones pick of Stone, Bronze, Pict, Scot or Druid ghost or any number of later versions. But we were not given time to visit any of these cairns or go on any ghost hunting expeditions, so we contented ourselves with exploring a very old graveyard containing a 'house of the dead'. This is just a small stone hut which was used, in years past, as a shelter by the relatives of the deceased. It was necessary for them to keep nightly vigils for some time after the burial in order to guard against grave snatchers, who sold the bodies to medical schools. There are many old, sculptured stones in this cemetery, some of them dating from the ninth century.

Since we did not raise any spirits from the dead at Kilmartin, we concentrated on raising our own spirits by breaking forth into song as we travelled along the road to Inveraray. This had an instant therapeutic effect upon us all, for acting as a counter irritant, it completely banished the hang-over of morbidity which prevailed after Kilmartin.

After lunch at the George Hotel, we visited Inveraray Castle, the home of the Duke of Argyll, Chieftain of the Clan Campbell. A certain part of this castle is open to the public.

By this time I was becoming a little blasé about castles so I decided that it was time to relegate them to the mental limbo of the lochs; in short to dump them all in the lochs and forget about them.

On the way back we stopped at St. Conan's Church, a unique and historic church, beautifully situated on the banks of Loch Watchumacallit. The church is quite impressive with its huge stone pillars. Near the sanctuary there are special seats reserved for the V.I.Ps, of the congregation, and their names were suitably inscribed thereon. I hope that I shall be forgiven if I was in any way sacriligious at the time for I have to confess that I sat in the seat of The MacDougall of Lorne.

The following day we had nothing special planned so we roamed around Oban. In the morning we visited a woollen mills just on the outskirts of the town. Here we saw the wool as it came from the sheep's back, washed, dyed, carded, spun and woven into scarves, tams, kilts, sweaters and socks *ad infinitum.*

In the course of watching all these processes, I became mixed up a bit in my directions, so I inquired from a young fellow who was working there just how I could get out of the place. "Lady," he said, "I have been working here for seven years and I haven't been able to get out yet."

In the afternoon we wandered up the hill and investigated the structure known as McCaig's Folly, which dominates the town. It reminds you of a Roman arena, circular in shape and surrounded by a huge stone wall broken by about fifty pointed arches. It was never completed as the builder ran out of funds. But it was rather pleasant to sit on a bench in the centre of this 'whatever it is' and view Oban Harbour through one of the archways.

This was our last day in Oban after a wonderful week. Sometime I hope to return to this little town for a more leisurely visit.

The next day we were off to Glasgow, where we rejoined our friends and after an overnight stay in that city, we took a final fling at Scotland – a Highland fling as it were. We had booked this tour when we had first arrived in the country – a seven day tour to Strathpeffer.

Northward we went once more, through Balloch and then along the bonnie banks of Loch Lomond and through progressively more rugged country until we reached Glencoe, a place whose very name has sinister connotations. As we came through the Pass of Glencoe, forbidding looking mountains rose all around us; but it was almost noon and the sun was shining and after all, a place cannot mourn forever. The doings which took place there three centuries ago receded to the background, especially after we were served an excellent lunch at the local hotel.

It developed as time went on that this particular tour really catered to its passengers; we were booked for the week at a luxury hotel, and during our day excursions, stops for lunch and afternoon tea were made at the very best places available. So for the ensuing week our major occupation, apart from sightseeing, was eating. I discovered that it is best not to request a glass of water with your meals as it seems to upset the whole establishment. You soon learn to do as the natives do and use water externally only. But there is no scarcity of other drinks, especially alcoholic ones.

After pondering and studying this problem in depth, namely the scarcity of drinking water versus the availability of Scotch, I arrived at the inevitable and logical conclusion that the rivers of Scotland have in their waters a certain alcoholic content.

This is a theory that would, no doubt, be sternly repudiated by all native Scotsmen. The fact of the matter is that it is a closely guarded secret for the whole economy of the nation would be disrupted should it become known abroad that its rivers are alcoholic. The breweries and distilleries, which are scattered all over the country, use this water and thus have a head start in the production of liquor.

Indeed it was confided to us by a new-found friend, a native of Scotland, that good whiskey depends to a certain extent on the water that is used, and that certain rivers are especially good as the water is filtered by nature through peat marshes, which contributes to the excellence of the ultimate product. I would go a little further and say that the process of fermentation *started* in the peat moorlands and hence the alcoholic content of the rivers.

An unbiased study of these rivers and streams would tend to confirm my theory. Scottish rivers do not meander peacefully and soberly along their courses; they leap and jump, they fall and tumble, they roar and gyrate, they are noisy and effervescent; in short, they are tipsy.

Again vast hydro-electric developements have been constructed throughout Scotland. One at Loch Sloy was pointed out to us as we went by. It was one of the largest in the country. A few days later, when we visited Glen Affric, we passed another huge hydro-electric scheme which was completed a few years ago.

These alco-hydro developements, in conjunction with the breweries and distilleries, constitute an immense system designed to take full advantage of Scotland's greatest natural asset – its water.

It is obvious that even the plant life is affected by its liquid intake and not always favourably. For instance, what did destroy the great Caledonian forests that centuries ago covered all of Scotland? Could it be that the trees slowly succumbed to chronic alcoholism?

As I mentioned previously in connection with Government reforestration, everywhere you can see orderly rows of pine and fir trees walking the straight and narrow path up the side of the mountain; but how long will they be able to resist the insidious and demoralizing effect of the water? Will they fall by the wayside?

Actually I saw only one tree which seemed to be definitely under the influence and not just a borderline case. Its appearance was so unusual, with its branches curled up and waving in a sort of loose-gestured and slap-happy fashion at all passers that I enquired the name and was told that it was the monkey puzzle tree.

After a little research I discovered that it was a species of pine and was a native of Chile. I had never seen such a tree before, not even in its native habitat. The fact that I have never been to Chile may, however, have some bearing on my failure to see it there.

I could enumerate quite a few other facts which would tend to confirm my theory but I will content myself with mentioning one more, namely Loch Ness, which we were now approaching. The thing that impressed me most about this loch, apart from its reputed denizen, was the fact that it had never been known to freeze. When you consider that it is in about the same latitude as Labrador, this would be difficult to explain; but if my theory is accepted then the explanation is very simple, namely – alcohol freezes at a lower temperature than water.

This loch is about 900 feet deep and apparently has an automatic heating system with thermostat located somewhere in connection with it, for it maintains a temperature of 32 degrees both summer and winter. It is the longest fresh water lake in Scotland and is two miles longer than Loch Lomond.

On the shores of the loch we saw a small yellow submarine which was brought over from the States by an American. For some weeks he had been engaged in a search for the elusive monster but with limited success.

Scientists also had an observation post set up commanding a view of the loch, and equipped with all modern aids, they had kept a twenty-four hour a day vigil throughout the summer.

As we travelled along the north-west shore of Loch Ness we viewed the Urquhart Castle, which is beautifully situated on a headland of the loch. It is off this headland that the monster is accustomed to disport or cavort or do his thing (as they say today).

While our coach stopped for a brief interval to enable us to look around, I had the following remarkable experience which I have entitled simply:

AN ICHTHYOSAURIAN EPISODE

Never till the day I die
Will I forget that baleful eye,
Draped around with water-cress
Staring at me from Loch Ness.

"Convolutions without number"

Closer scrutiny revealed
A mighty head but half concealed,
While far away a tail was found
That apparently belonged.

Keeping head and tail asunder
Convolutions without number
Lengthened out across the bay,
(Overdoing it I'd say).

Such an elongated torso
Covered half a mile or moreso;
When he wished to flip his tail
Word was sent out by air-mail.

On his head he wore a Stetson,
Salvaged from some flot and jetsam;
In the region of his middle
Hung an ancient Celtic fiddle.

Which he strummed with gay abandon
Hitting all the notes at random;
Scales to him were element'ry
For they covered all his peltry.

Fellow tourists saw no trace
Of what stared them in the face;
Like a cosmic verity
He was far too big to see.

When they branded him a lie
He winked his periscopic eye
And with a snort of mild derision,
Vanished from my line of vision.

After all this business of castles and monsters, it was only fitting that at sundown we should arrive at an enchanted village, the village of Strathpeffer, where we were to make our headquarters for a week. It was not only enchanted but enchanting, a jewel of a place in a fairy tale setting. It nestled in a valley surrounded by mountains. From the hotel where we were staying we looked out at a magnificent view of Ben Wyvis and Little Wyvis. There may possibly have been quite a few others of the Wyvis family in the neighbourhood but these were the most notable members.

The only disconcerting thing about Strathpeffer was its name. It took me a whole week before I could pronounce the word without sneezing. Whether that phenomenon was due to association of ideas, namely with the word "pepper" or whether it was some sort of spell cast upon me by a local genie, I shall never know.

Apart from such occasional respiratory paroxysms, our stay in Strathpeffer was most delightful. It was a pleasant change to have everything mapped out for us, where to stay, what to do, when to eat and where, and at times what to say.

Some people might not appreciate this organized routine but we enjoyed it. It relieved us of the necessity of making decisions, a difficult thing at the best of times. So we devoted out energies exclusively to the enjoyment of the scenery and also to the entertainment provided.

There were interesting walks to take, golf to play and mineral waters to drink. Should one have a tendency to rheumatoid arthritis, perhaps aggravated by London fog or Edinburgh drizzle, then all one had to do was to drink the waters of the Spa and be cured. (What did I tell you about the water in Scotland?)

For evening entertainment we could see highland dancing in the village square or attend a Scottish cabaret in the concert hall. Here a most capable master of ceremonies would quickly put everybody into the spirit of the thing and before long we would all be contributing to the general amusement, heel and toeing, Highland flinging and Strathspeying with the best of them. "Are you having a good time?" called out the M.C. "Yes" was the unqualified reply. "Don't say 'yes' say 'ay-e'," said the M.C. So "ay-e" it was from then on.

The following days we sash-ayed back and forth across the Hielands of Scotland, visiting east and west coasts impartially from Dornoch, Cromarty and Fortrose on the east to Gairloch, Altbee and Ullapool on the west.

Many of the place names seemed very familiar as we have so many like names in Nova Scotia and especially Cape Breton. Dingwall, Inverness, Glencoe, Skye, Stirling, Glengarry and many more have their counterparts in our island.

I am grateful, however, that our Scottish ancestors had the good sense to leave behind them in their native land many place names which, to the uninitiated, are not only unpronounceable but at times unthinkable. Unlike "Strathpeffer" you cannot even sneeze them.

A mouth filled with oatmeal, I was given to understand, would help greatly in achieving the exact Gaelic inflection and intonation. This would necessitate carrying the oatmeal around at all times. Whenever it was felt that a word requiring special treatment was coming up, then some oatmeal would be popped into the mouth.

I tried this procedure out for several days with outstanding results. Words, which I had never been known to utter, now came quite easy to me. I will admit that there were some unfortunate side effects as I broke out in a rash and was obliged to resort to the waters of the Spa for relief.

In spite of the fact that both my maternal and paternal ancestors came from Scotland, it seems that I am allergic to two things, oatmeal and bagpipes. If I am subjected to either of them I break out in a dermatitic eruption. If I ate oatmeal porridge while the bagpipes were playing the result would probably be fatal.

Some places stand out in my memory; there was lovely Glen Affric and the serene Loch Beneveian. It was on the banks of this loch that my husband carefully gathered several varieties of heather, which still remained in bloom, with the idea of bringing them back home.

From then on that bunch of heather accompanied us in our travels. It was treated like a baby; it was watered, fed and at night put to bed carefully wrapped in a plastic bag and hung out the hotel window.

Although we were aware that the lynx-eyed Canadian customs officials would never tolerate its introduction into our fair Nova Scotia (something to do with hoof and mouth disease) nevertheless we toted it around hopefully, only to have it vanish while we were on our return trip across the Atlantic.

I did not particularly mourn its demise, especially when several weeks later I noticed that we had in our own garden a specimen or two almost identical to the heather.

Then there was Ullapool, a thriving fishing settlement wonderfully situated on Loch Broom amid superb scenery and 3,000 seagulls. Now gulls I love to watch as they wheel and soar, dive and dip with the quintessence of grace. From an aesthetic point of view they are marvellous, but from any other standpoint, especially if you are standing on the Quay Street in Ullapool, they are a direct menace.

How the natives manage to survive the constant aerial barrage I do not know. I admit that I did not see any direct hits, which fact may lend credence to the story that the gulls have been educated over the course of years to the point where they exercise care in their personal habits and deliberately avoid any human targets. But to believe this one may have to stretch one's gullibility a bit.

This place was of particular interest to my husband for it was from Loch Broom that his ancestors set sail for Nova Scotia on the ship *Hector* in the year 1773. On board the ship were some 189 passengers including 24 MacKays. On September 15th, 1773, the ship sailed into Pictou Harbour on the northern coast of Nova Scotia.

*The young men, arrayed in their kilts and their dirks, stood on the deck. As they entered the harbour the piper blew a full blast on his pipes. The Indians had been harassing the first settlers. Their warrior braves had feared not any man. But they fled in terror before the weird sound of the bag-pipes – and were not seen for some time.**

*Clara Dennis: *More About Nova Scotia,* p.125, The Ryerson Press Toronto, 1937.

The moral of the above story is that it is well not to underestimate the value of the bag-pipes as a weapon of aggression.

On the way back from Ullapool we stopped at the Corrieshalloch Gorge in order to obtain a view of the falls. There is a small platform projecting directly over the 200′ gorge and prominently displayed on it is the warning sign that two people only would be allowed on the platform at one time.

This figure was no doubt arrived at after a series of trial and error experiments. I can visualize them starting with about ten people, which would be the maximum number the space allowed. But as platform and people disappeared into the depths of the gorge, it would become obvious that they would have to try out nine people on a new platform the next day.

This process may seem a bit wasteful of human life and lumber, yet it exemplifies the modern scientific approach to learning. After a loss of 8 platforms and 52 lives the number *two* would be definitely established as the maximal safety factor.

This gorge was a mile long and it was really a gorgeous gorge. To obtain a better view of it we went across a foot-bridge which spanned the ravine. I know now why it is called a suspension bridge for actually the suspense is terrific. By the time my faltering steps had reached the centre, the bridge was swaying so much that I felt like the man on the flying trapeze who was just learning his act.

I ultimately reached the opposite side and terra firma only to be immediately confronted with the necessity of a return trip back to firma terra. I would have gone down on my hands and knees and crawled back, were it not for the fact that I had irrevocably given up this means of locomotion when I was 11 months old; besides it would be difficult to maintain the dignity compatible with my age while down on all fours.

In times of great stress my mind invariably ceases to function (this often happens at other times too) so how I made the return trip will always remain a mystery. I was told later that the view from the bridge was spectacular.

Another particularly interesting place was the Inverewe Gardens. These were started over a century ago by an enterprising Scotsman, Osgood MacKenzie. They have now been taken over by the National Trust for Scotland and are visited annually by thousands of people from all over the world.

Mr. MacKenzie, who seemed to have a flair for doing the impossible, decided to plant a garden on the side of a barren mountain. This was, I was told, a portion of the Torridon range, the oldest mountain range in the world. There was no soil, the Torridon skeletal framework being covered with peat varying from an inch to several feet.

Therefore soil had to be carried up the hillside in creels. But first of all trees had to be planted as wind-breaks and at times there was a pitched battle between wind and trees to determine which would break which. But the plant kingdom eventually won out and today you can see there specimens of shrubs and trees from every country in the world.

In this northern latitude of approximately 58 degrees, corresponding to that of the tip of Greenland, one is amazed to find thriving palm trees and plantations of bamboo. (This particular area is known as Bambooselem). Of course, Mr. MacKenzie had a certain amount of cooperation from the Gulf Stream which was accommodating enough to bathe this western coast and prevent any really severe frosts.

It is my personal conviction that if a Scotsman were marooned on an ice floe in the Arctic Ocean, he would sooner or later achieve a quite creditable garden there.

One day, while on our way back from Dornoch, we followed the Shin River to the Shin Falls, which is famous for its salmon leap. We were rewarded by seeing dozens of salmon attempting to leap up the falls, although many were thrown back by the terrific force of the water.

I felt that we should lend a helping hand or fin or something but seemingly they preferred to make it on their own, so we left them battling almost impossible odds.

Our sojourn in Scotland was all too brief. Although we had covered a great deal in the short time at our disposal, there was a lot more that we had not seen. I would have liked to have given more time to a study of the flora and fauna as well as to the finna of the Hielands but that will have to be postponed to a future date. So I left with the conviction that anything after Scotland was bound to be an anti-climax.

We had reservations by Aer Lingus to Dublin so on the final day of our tour we arrived back in Glasgow with the intention of boarding the plane in an hour or so, but when we arrived at the Glasgow airport we discovered that all planes were grounded due to a strike. Over there they call them "lightning strikes". They go into effect without warning and for any specified time – it may be for 2 hours or 24 hours or more. There is always the delightful element of surprise, a strike may pop up at any time.

Recalling our experience on the train when our waiters vanished without a trace in the act of serving us high tea, I am inclined to believe that that, also, was due to a lightning strike.

So there we were at Glasgow Airport wandering around in the hopes of encountering someone who could direct us to Ireland. The place seemed to be completely deserted of all air-port personnel, but eventually someone, who seemed to be in the know, suggested that we take a bus to Prestwick Airport, a distance of about 35 miles.

We followed his advice and, as there was no strike on, lightning or otherwise, at that airport, we soon boarded an Aer Lingus plane and without further incident took off for Dublin.

My first impression of the plane was that it looked a little bit the worse for wear. It had that rather weary look as though it might have been suffering from metal fatigue. I hoped that it could get us across the Irish Sea before it succumbed to whatever was ailing it.

I diligently read all the safety instructions as to how to fasten on the parachute and what emergency exit to take, although I knew perfectly well that, should any crisis arise, I would immediately freeze into petrified immobility and my mind would cease even its normal lethargic functioning.

It did not lessen my apprehension to find a prayer inserted along with the safety folder. But I read it through reverently and, as it developed later on, it was most efficacious for we arrived safely at Dublin Airport after about an hour's flight.

There is one suggestion, however, that I intend to

submit to the management of the airline and it is this: there should be a clause inserted in the prayer to cover baggage – a sort of extended coverage at it were. I have always found that when praying for something it pays to be specific, otherwise although your prayer is answered, it may not be exactly what you had in mind.

In this particular instance when we prayed for a safe journey we made no mention of our luggage, so when we went to claim our bags we discovered that a handle had disassociated itself from one bag and they were no longer going around together. Now how to carry a flight bag without a handle presents a problem especially when the bag has been distended to its full capacity.

My suggestion to my husband that he unfold it and wrap it around himself in the manner of an out-size life belt did not meet with any enthusiasm on his part. He ended up by grabbing it and clutching it to his chest in an ecstatic embrace. To any interested bystander, and there were quite a few, it would appear that he had quite recently held up a bank and was making sure that nobody would lay hands on the swag.

It was late, nearly midnight, and when we emerged from the terminal we discovered that it was raining. We were all tired as it had been a long day of travelling from Strathpeffer (excuse me while I sneeze) and we were all in a rather snappish mood.

Fortunately we had reservations at Jury's Hotel, otherwise we might have had to sit on the curb for the night. We found out the following day that every hotel and tourist lodge was booked to the limit for the week-end due to a football game which was scheduled for Saturday afternoon.

As a result all Eire was converging on Dublin and everyone was in high spirits and, conversely, high spirits were in everyone. For myself, I prefer non-alcoholic beverages so I confined myself to coffee – Irish coffee – and discovered that the Irish make a really excellent and very stimulating brew.

The following morning we set out to explore Dublin, which proved a fascinating city with religious overtones. Church bells pealed the Angelus, announced the various masses and at times, I am inclined to believe, rang for no particular reason but just out of sheer exuberance of spirits.

Taxi drivers blessed themselves as they passed a church, and a man on the street crossed himself as an ambulance went by. I found myself becoming imbued with the religious spirit and was considering blessing myself before attempting to cross at a very busy intersection, but I decided that that was leaning a bit too heavily on the Almighty, when I should be able to negotiate it on my own.

That was a mistake for I found myself stranded at the junction of five streets converging at impossible angles and I was in the centre with traffic flowing all around me. I might at this point state that the concept of chivalry had died a natural death, as far as my husband was concerned, when we had first encountered London traffic. From then on it was each one for himself.

So in this particular instance, he and our friends were blithely and unconcernedly disappearing from view around a corner, while I was left standing there in a state of ossification.

Then I heard the siren of an ambulance and that

ululant sound itself is enough to strike terror into your heart. I am convinced that no mechanical contrivance could emit such blood-curdling wails from a Dublin ambulance, I can only conclude that the City fathers inveigled or coerced some of their native Banshees, who are well known for their talents along these lines, to enroll in the ambulance service, and the result is a howling success.

The thought occurred to me as I stood there, that they were almost too efficient in arriving with an ambulance as, as yet, I was not even a casualty. But the ambulance passed me by missing me by inches.

By this time I was probably considered one of the permanent fixtures of the Square; one of those grotesque statues which you see set up in improbable places for no obvious reason. While I envisioned myself standing there forever, with the moss growing on my north side, suddenly and inexplicably there was a lull in traffic. I took immediate advantage of it and springing with the grace and agility of a mountain goat, I reached the opposite side and safety.

That evening as we sauntered around the City, we found ourselves the recipients of a quite unsolicited cleaning service. At a fountain in one of the Squares a crowd of football celebrants, all in the spirit of good clean fun, had dumped a quantity of detergent in the fountain and were then busily engaged in cleaning up the world, including themselves and all passers-by.

Language was no problem in Ireland as we found it, at times, in Scotland and even in England. Although in Eire the Government has made Gaelic the state language and you hear it on the streets, yet everyone speaks English, especially to tourists. Incidentally, slight knowledge of Gaelic stood me in good stead.

Phrases such as "camera how" and "clay va" were familiar to me from my childhood.

All signs were in Gaelic and place names had been changed to their Gaelic counterparts. Thus Killarney was shown as Cill Aernai at the railway station. The signs on the rest rooms were FIR and MNA. Some author, whose book I read recently, gave some valuable information when he stated that the way to remember which was which was to think of MNA as "Men not allowed". The Lord only knows what FIR means.

Speaking of rest rooms, here in Canada there is strict segregation of the sexes, but in Britain you run into, and I do mean run, all sorts and varieties of places, some completely asexual, such as on the train from London. At one quite posh hotel in Scotland the doors on the upstairs rest rooms bore the unassuming and simple inscription "W.C." whereas downstairs there were most elaborate powder rooms and lavatories.

In one hotel I noticed the signs "Ladies", "Gentlemen" and a third with just "Toilet". That last was probably reserved for those of indeterminate sex. Today there seemed to be quite a few people who are unable to classify themselves in the first two categories.

In some really de luxe places you get toilet tissue that is truly effective for the purpose for which it was designed but, for the most part, the tissue has the effect of fine sand paper. The abrasive action on the British posteriors over a period of years must be tremendous. It would have to be seen to be believed.

A deposit of one English penny will generally admit

you to a rest-room. These pennies are large, cumbersome coins and are of no monetary value (as I will explain later) but it is advisable to carry a number of them at all times for the afore-mentioned reason, especially if you are afflicted with a bladder condition.

Now for a word or two about the British currency which might prove helpful as a guide for prospective travellers. We shall consider first the various coins and their value in American money.

		Value
Crown	this coin is non-existent and therefore can have no value	0
Half-Crown	the equivalent of 2s 6d is equal to one half of nothing (also non-existent)	0
Florin	worth 2 shillings is obviously less than a half crown or less then nothing	0
Shilling	worth 1/2 a florin or one half of nothing	0
Penny	1/12 of shilling, considerably less than nothing	0
Half-Penny	or Haepenny is 1/24th of a shilling and what can you do with that?	0
Pound	This is known by the sign L with a stroke through it and is not the sort of thing that you go on a diet to lose. It equals 20s which is 20 x 0	0

The above figures represent the value in U.S. money. For Canadian money the value would be slightly less depending on the rate of exchange.

In spite of the lack of monetary value, the British seem quite attached to those coins and actually prefer them to real money so it is best to humour them and keep a supply on hand.

Since writing the above I learned that the British

are scrapping this monetary system and a new one will prevail, beginning in February 1970. Some astute mathematician, after years of laborious research, no doubt arrived at the same results as I have outlined above and, realizing the futility of the system, decided to replace it.

My only regret is that it did not happen sooner as it would have saved me a lot of mental wear and tear – in other words my efforts all came to naught (0).

A day or two later we arrived at Killarney after a train trip there from Dublin. These radio train excursions are quite pleasant. The passengers are regaled *en route* with Irish music, Irish coffee, jokes and commentaries on places of interest.

As our fare included a jaunting car trip around the Lakes, we thought it well to get our money's worth even though the day was chilly. Now these jaunting cars are anything but jaunty. They seem to have the uncanny knack of reducing to the lowest common denominator all who ride on them.

As I paused at the station, waiting for my husband to emerge from the FIR, I had a chance to observe the amazing metamorphosis which took place in a person the minute he or she stepped aboard. The effect was due partly to the fact everyone was swathed in blankets which had been supplied by the driver and most women wore a scarf or kerchief on the head, completing the peasant effect.

The seats were high and narrow (in my case I almost needed a derrick to be put in position) and there were two rows facing the sides of the road. For the first few miles I felt very insecure and expected to fall off with the slightest bump.

It was a ten mile drive around the Lakes. In spite of the blanket I found myself slowly congealing as the weary horse jogged along the dirt road. In my semi-frigid state it was a bit difficult to appreciate fully the beauty of the scenery for it was truly very lovely and unspoiled. It would have been more enjoyable if those in charge had turned the thermostat up a few notches.

The vegetation around the Lakes was luxuriant and semi-tropical. There were palm trees in evidence, rhododendrons seemed to be growing everywhere, although there was only an occasional bloom on them at that time of the year. We glimpsed a red deer in the thicket, but we did not have the pleasure of meeting any leprechauns or little people even though the terrain would appear to be an ideal setting for them.

The closely woven growth of vines, shrubs and roots of upturned trees formed small, dark recesses and caves which had a very sinister look and which could house anything imaginable, natural or supernatural. At any rate I will not discount the leprechaun story even though I did not see one. After all I am willing to concede that there are no snakes in Ireland even though I saw one. One must be logical.

I meant to tell you about the snake business before. One of the things which we saw in Dublin and which I recall very vividly was something that does not even exist in Ireland today; they were all driven out by St. Patrick centuries ago. It was only a small snake but nevertheless a snake and as emerald green as the island is reputed to be. It was a bit sluggish as the morning was cold, but when my husband touched it with his foot, it disappeared into a nearby hedge. There may not be snakes in Ireland but there is at least *one* snake.

"... there are no snakes in Ireland ... they were all driven out by St. Patrick."

My husband was tactless enough to bring up this subject of conversation with the driver of the jaunting car, telling him the story in detail. The driver, who hitherto had been a most loquacious and entertaining fellow, suddenly lapsed into complete silence, obviously stricken to the core. One of his most cherished beliefs had been assailed and lay crumbling at his feet and there was nothing he could do or say.

I was relieved when we returned to our starting point and found that there was still a modicum of sensation in my limbs. Fortunately there was a tea-room handy, so two pots of tea later I was beginning to thaw out from the deep freeze and feel a returning interest in life.

We found the Irish people very friendly, outgoing, and helpful. If you should happen to ask directions from a bystander, he would be quite liable to walk along with you and give you a personally conducted tour of the City. From taxi and courier drivers we obtained valuable information that we would never have gained otherwise.

For instance, when we asked whether any heather grew in Ireland, we were informed that many years ago the hills were covered with heather but that they had, unfortunately, exported it all to Scotland. As I had always presumed that heather was native to Scotland, it was therefore a revelation to find that it was merely an import from Ireland. There are any number of facts such as this, which you will not find in text books, which make travel in Ireland so educational.

But apart from the educational, there was the Irish Cabaret at our hotel which provided a memorable evening of sparkling entertainment, with Irish songs and dances featured and a harpist who must have played on the harp "that once through Tara's halls the soul of music played".

The master of ceremonies for the evening combined the roles of chairman and magician. In the latter capacity he performed some quite amazing feats of legerdemain with an invisible deck of cards. As we had never seen such a deck before we were naturally very much intrigued.

We happened to be seated near the stage so the magician asked my husband if he would be kind enough to shuffle the deck for him and pick out a card, etc. This my husband was quite willing to do. Imagine his surprise at the end of the performance, when the magician presented him with the invisible deck of cards as a reward for his assistance, and as a souvenir of the evening.

I had some doubt whether he should have accepted the cards as they were, no doubt, quite valuable and moreover, there might be difficulty getting them through Customs. However, we were assured that they would be duty free, as, indeed, we found them to be when we declared them upon our arrival in Halifax.

The deck of cards is now among the most cherished mementoes of our trip. We are always very proud to show it to our friends who are duly impressed by its total invisibility. True, we occasionally encounter a sceptic but then you will find those in every walk of life.

On a coach trip to Glendalough we had the opportunity of seeing a lovely section of Eire as we traversed the southern shore route. As usual our driver courier enlivened our trip with anecdotes and commentaries on the countryside. As we passed the smallest village in Eire, consisting solely of a school, a church and a house (in which the mayor lived), we were told that in that little school no less than five bishops had received their education. We were all suitably impressed until he added: "There was Molly Bishop, Terence, Kevin, Paddy and Eileen Bishop."

We then went inland to the Vale of Glendalough. Here we looked over the ruins of the monastery and chapels founded in the sixth century by Saint Kevin. This place was one of the most renowned centres of learning in Europe at one time. I could not help but be struck by the contrast between this lush, beautiful valley, protected by the surrounding mountains which St. Kevin picked for his monastery, and the harsh, bleak Iona shores selected by St. Columba.

Time was not available after lunch for very much exploration; our driver was not inclined to let us dally unduly, especially when there was a stop scheduled at a singing pub further along the road.

There are not too many of those singing pubs left so I understand; which fact might be considered regrettable by those who like to join in the fun and raise their voices in song while enjoying their favourite drink. As a chap at the piano banged out familiar Irish airs and songs of the first world war vintage it was hard not to join in and add to the general discord. But it might prove a knock-out blow from which the singing pubs might never rise again.

The following day we returned to London where we planned to devote a little time to stores and theatres before making our homeward flight.

While shopping in one large department store I came across an art exhibit where a number of oil paintings were displayed. The artist was from Wales and the scenes were of his native country. It suddenly occurred to me that I had overlooked Wales in our travels so I decided to make partial amends by taking something of that country home with us, so I purchased one of the paintings.

That sounds as though the transaction was completed in five minutes, but actually it took the greater part of the afternoon. Although I was reasonably sure that original paintings come into Canada duty free, nevertheless it was thought necessary to phone the Canadian Embassy to verify the fact. As the assistant carefully wrapped the picture, which seemed to take an endless time, I got into conversation with the lady in charge. It developed that we had something in common as she was a native of Scotland.

When I volunteered the information that my ancestors had been driven out in the Clearances, she replied "Ay-e a dreadful thing, the Clearances." Before long we were practically weeping on each others shoulders as we went back in history about 200 years to the time when our forefathers were weighed in the balance with sheep and found wanting. When she learned my name was MacKay, her comment was "A vurry well thought of clan" which, coming from her, I considered high praise.

One would expect that in London where English is presumably spoken we would have no language difficulties. But the majority of the people with whom we came in contact daily, such as waiters, seemed to be foreign and more especially Greek. They barely understood us and we could not understand them at all. Xenephon's *Anabasis*, to which I was given a hurried introduction during my school years, did not equip me to order ham and eggs in Greek.

It is a curious anomaly that in Eire, where the official language is Gaelic, we had no trouble as everyone spoke our own brand of English. In Scotland, where we would expect to feel more at home, we were at times mystified by some of their phrases; and in England, Cockney was quite incomprehensible on occasions.

Someone had recommended that we see a certain play, a comedy which was then running in London. Most of the characters in the play spoke Cockney while the remaining ones spoke with an impeccable Oxford accent and we found both equally confusing.

We sensed that there was a lot of sparkling repartee, to judge from the laughter of the audience, but most of it was lost on us. Occasionally, as the gist of a joke finally percolated through our mental fog, we emitted a delayed reaction of laughter. This only evoked curious stares from those in our vicinity, who by that had gone on to something quite serious.

However, I enjoyed it in my own peculiar fashion and in spite of the fact that I was suffering from a severe case of the sniffles, a hang-over from our jaunting car trip to Cill Aernai.

Well, our time was running out and the next morning we were back at the London Airport preparatory to taking off for Nova Scotia. While I was making a few last minute purchases at the souvenir shop, my husband joined a long queue in front of the liquor store. The fact that we were allowed to take back with us two 40 ounce bottles of liquor duty free was much too much for any red-blooded man to resist.

When our flight was announced he was still far down the line and moving very slowly forward. A few minutes later a second announcement came over the loudspeaker, requesting all passengers on flight 603 for Halifax to report immediately at Gate 12 as the plane was ready to depart.

I was beginning to get frantic and tried to persuade him to forget about the liquor, but as he had already paid for it, the thought of leaving it unclaimed went against everything in his Scottish make-up. So he resolutely moved forward by inches while a third announcement was made. This time they practically entreated the remaining four passengers, meaning ourselves and our friends to board the plane.

At last we made a dash for it, my husband triumphantly carrying two bottles of Scotch in one hand and his precious bunch of heather along with an Edinburgh haggis in the other. As there was no time to rearrange burdens, I was weighed down with everything else, including umbrella, camera, handbag, top coat and my oil painting which seemed to have somehow grown in size since I bought it. But we made it; everyone else was seated in the plane as we jostled down the length of the aisle.

I had some idea that now that we had arrived, like royalty, the plane would take off immediately, but actually we waited – and waited; some delay due to fueling, so they said.

When I picked up a London newspaper and started to read the headlines, I discovered the real reason for the delay. It seems that there had been a theft of a very valuable painting on the previous day. The police were watching all airports as they suspected an attempt would be made to smuggle it out of the country. They had undoubtedly seen me carrying a large picture and had notified Scotland Yard. The officials were probably on their way to the Airport then.

Although I knew that I could establish my complete innocence, nevertheless, it would be a most embarrassing situation in front of my friends. The stigma would likely mark me for the remainder of my life. I could hear the story being repeated as it improved with years: "Would you believe that she was involved in a big international art swindle? Yes, she was smuggling fabulous art treasures across the border. Scotland Yard was on her trail and nearly nabbed her once but she got away."

As I was musing in this vein, I suddenly realized that we were airborne. England was slipping away from under us and we were homeward bound, after a most memorable cruise. As in the wanderings of Ulysses I had seen many unusual things, *mirabile dictu,* including monsters of the deep, enchanted castles, snakes that did not exist, a fabulous smoo and reeling rivers.

But I mentioned none of these things to the lady who sat next to me. When she asked me whether I enjoyed my trip, I responded with a heartfelt and emphatic "Ay-e, that I did."

The Captain's voice came over the loudspeaker: "We are now cruising at an altitude of 30,000 feet." The bar was now opened; champagne was flowing like the River Spean in spate and the noise rose by decibels. I settled back in my seat and completely relaxed for the first time in weeks, as once again we were flying high.